Will The Real Heretics Please Stand Up

A New Look at Today's Evangelical Church in the Light of Early Christianity

David W. Bercot

SCROLL
PUBLISHING

ISBN: 092-4722-002

Library of Congress Catalog No. 89-090677

Cover design: R. Miller

Printed in the United States of America

To my loving wife,
Deborah

Contents

1

The Prisoner

As the chariot rumbled through the stone-paved streets of Smyrna, the prisoner could already hear the roar of the frenzied crowd in the arena. Scavenger dogs followed the chariot through the streets, barking wildly. Olive-skinned children scurried out of the way, their eyes wide with excitement. Nameless faces peered out of windows along the street.

Halting outside the massive walls of the arena, the guard brusquely dumped the prisoner out of the chariot as though he were a sack of garbage, injuring the prisoner's leg.

For weeks, the public had clamored for this man's arrest and execution. But he hardly looked like a dangerous criminal—a frail old man, his face etched with wrinkles. His hair and beard were as white as the clouds that dotted the Mediterranean sky that afternoon. As the aged prisoner limped into the arena under armed guard, word quickly spread through the crowds that this was Polycarp—the vile criminal whose death they had come to see. His crime? He was the local leader of the superstitious cult known as the Christians.

As the crowd roared with bloodthirsty excitement, the soldiers led the prisoner to the stand where the Roman proconsul was seated. As the proconsul stared at the limping old man, his face flushed with embarrassment. So this was the dangerous criminal who had caused such an uproar! Just a gentle old man.

1

The proconsul, his purple robe flapping in the breeze, leaned forward in his seat and privately addressed the elderly prisoner, saying, "The Roman government doesn't make war on old men. Simply swear by the divinity of Caesar, and I'll let you go."

"I can't do that."

"Well, then, simply shout, 'Away with the atheists,' and that will be sufficient." (Since the Christians had no temples or images of any god, many Romans assumed they were atheists.)

The prisoner calmly stretched out his wrinkled arm and turned in a circle with a sweeping gesture toward the hate-filled crowd. Gazing intently toward heaven, he shouted, "Away with the atheists!"

The proconsul was momentarily taken aback by the prisoner's response. Though he had done what was commanded, the proconsul knew from the reaction of the crowd that he dare not release Polycarp yet.

"Curse Jesus Christ!" he demanded.

For a few moments, Polycarp stared with his piercing brown eyes into the stern countenance of the proconsul. He then replied calmly, "For eighty-six years I've served Jesus, and he has never wronged me in any way. How, then, can I possibly curse my very King and Savior?"

The crowd, unable to hear the conversation, was growing impatient with the delay. So the proconsul anxiously urged the prisoner again, "Swear by the divinity of Caesar!"

"Since you keep pretending that you don't know what I am, let me simplify your task. I declare without shame that I am a Christian. If you'd like to learn what Christians believe, set a time and I will tell you."

Fidgeting nervously, the proconsul blurted back, "Don't try to persuade *me*, persuade *them*," pointing to the crowd.

Polycarp glanced at the faceless mob who were eagerly waiting for their bloody entertainment to begin. "No, I won't cheapen the teachings of Jesus by trying to persuade such a throng."

The proconsul shouted angrily back, "Don't you know I have wild animals at my disposal? I will unleash them on you immediately unless you repent!"

"Well then, unleash them," Polycarp replied. There was no fear in his voice. "Whoever heard of repenting from what is good in order to follow what is evil?"

The proconsul was accustomed to intimidating even the strongest, most hardened criminals, but this old man was getting the best of him. He lashed back at the prisoner, "Since wild animals don't seem to scare you, know here and now that I will have you burned alive if you don't immediately denounce this Jesus Christ!"

Infused with the Holy Spirit, Polycarp was now beaming with joy and confidence. "You threaten me with a mere fire that burns for an hour and then goes out. Haven't you heard of the fire of coming judgment and of the eternal punishment reserved for the ungodly? Why do you keep delaying? Do whatever you want with me."

It wasn't supposed to have worked this way. The proconsul was supposed to be the mighty conqueror, with the prisoner on his knees begging for mercy. But this prisoner—an old man—had vanquished the proconsul. The proconsul sank back into his seat in humiliating defeat.

Because of the vastness of the stadium, heralds were sent to several different stations throughout the arena to announce what Polycarp had said. When his final statement was announced, a wave of fury swept the crowd. They would do with him what *they* wanted! Screaming for Polycarp's death, they spilled out of their seats into the corridors and through the exits. Running wildly through the city streets, they gathered wood from wherever they could find it. They looted stores and even stole the firewood piled inside the public baths. Then they thronged back into the arena, their arms laden with fuel for the executioner's pyre. They piled the wood around an upright stake, to which the soldiers began to nail Polycarp's limbs.

However, he calmly assured the soldiers, "Leave me as I am. The one who gives me the strength to endure the fire will also enable me to remain motionless against the stake without having to be secured." After allowing Polycarp to pray, the soldiers lit the wood.

By burning Polycarp, the people of Smyrna thought they would blot out his name forever and bring an end to the hated superstition called Christianity. But like the proconsul, they grossly underestimated the vitality and conviction of the Christians. Rather than intimidating other Christians, the death of Polycarp inspired them. Rather than disappearing, Christianity grew.

Ironically, what the Romans couldn't accomplish was eventually accomplished by professing Christians themselves. Today, the name of Polycarp has been largely forgotten, and the Christianity of his day is unknown to most westerners.

2

Who Were The Early Christians?

I still remember my college English professor trying to impress on me the importance of defining my terms in my essays. Although I gave little heed to his words at the time, I realized the significance of his admonition when I began discussing the early Christians with various groups. Invariably, one of the first questions people ask me is: "Just who do you mean by 'the early Christians'?"

So let me define some terms. By the term "early Christians," I am primarily referring to the Christians who lived between 90 and 199 A.D. The Apostle John was still living at the beginning of this period. The first generation of early Christians were men like Polycarp who had been personally taught by one or more of the apostles. The period ended with a man who was only one human link removed from John—Irenaeus, a pupil of Polycarp.

By the term "early Christianity," I am referring to beliefs and practices of the world-wide community of early Christians who maintained bonds of fellowship and communion with each other. I'm not referring to the beliefs or practices of anyone labeled as a heretic by that church. So I'm not describing the entire field of wheat and weeds mixed together, but only the wheat (Matt. 13:24-30).[1]

5

Although this book primarily focuses on the Christians who lived between 90 and 199, the common beliefs and practices of these early Christians were generally maintained by Christians living in the next century. For that reason, the discussion that follows will also include quotations from writers who lived between 200 and 313, as long as their teachings agree with those who lived in the period immediately after the apostles.

Were These The "Early Church Fathers?"

When I start talking about the early Christian writers, people usually respond by saying, "Oh, you mean the early church fathers." *But these men were not church fathers!* Most of them were fairly ordinary, hard-working Christian leaders with above-average education. They would have been highly indignant at being called "church fathers." The only "church fathers" they recognized were the apostles.

Actually, the very fact that these writers were *not* church fathers is what makes their writings so valuable. If these men had been great founders of theology, their writings would be of limited value to us. They would simply tell us what doctrines these particular "founding theologians" had developed. But these men did not write theological treatises. In fact, no one in the second century church can even be called a theologian in the modern sense. And there is no real systematic theology in the entire pre-Constantine church.

Instead, the early Christian writings primarily consist of: (1) apologetic works explaining universally-held Christian beliefs to the Romans and Jews; (2) works defending apostolic Christianity against heretics; and (3) correspondence between churches. These writings are a witness to what the church in general believed and practiced during the period shortly after the apostles had died. This is what makes them invaluable.

In fact, the only person during the entire period between 90 and 313 who can rightly be called a theologian is Origen. But Origen didn't impose his views on other Christians. Instead, he was one of the least dogmatic of all the writers of the early Christian period. And this was an age when nobody was very dogmatic on matters beyond the relatively few essential Christian doctrines.

One of the noticeable features of early Christianity is the relative lack of rigidly-defined theological dogma. In fact, the further one goes back in Christian history, the less defined dogma he finds. Nevertheless, there still were some essential doctrines and common practices that all orthodox Christians held to. This book will focus on these common or universally-held beliefs and practices.

To that end, I have not represented any beliefs or practices as being those of the early church in general unless they met the following criteria:

- All early Christian writers who mentioned the subject expressed the same view; and
- At least five early Christian writers, separated by time or geographical distance, discussed the subject.

Actually, most of the matters discussed in this book are supported by testimony from more than five writers.

A Brief Introduction
To 8 Major Writers

Before discussing the early Christian teachings, I want to first introduce you to some of the writers from whom I will be primarily quoting:

Polycarp—Disciple of the Apostle John

Polycarp *(POL ih karp),* whose death was described earlier, was a model of faith and devotion to congregations in Asia. He was a personal companion and disciple of the Apostle John, who evidently appointed him overseer or bishop of the congregation at Smyrna.[2] If the "angels" of the seven churches of Revelation refer to the overseers of those churches, then it's quite possible that the "angel" of the church of Smyrna was none other than Polycarp. If so, this is noteworthy because Smyrna is one of the two churches in Revelation for which Jesus had no words of rebuke.

Polycarp lived until he was at least 87. He was finally martyred around 155 A.D.

Irenaeus—The Crucial Human Link to the Apostles

One of Polycarp's personal disciples was Irenaeus *(EAR reh NAY us),* who moved to Gaul (France) to serve as a missionary. When the overseer of the congregation in Lyons, France, was killed during persecution, Irenaeus was named as his successor. The entire early church spoke well of Irenaeus, and he lived past 200 A.D. As a pupil of Polycarp, who was a companion of the Apostle John, Irenaeus served as an important human link to the age of the apostles.

Justin—Philosopher Turned Evangelist

During Polycarp's lifetime, a young philosopher named Justin *(JUS tin)* embarked on a spiritual journey to find truth. One day, he was walking to his accustomed place of meditation in a secluded field overlooking the Mediterranean. Suddenly, he noticed an old man walking at a distance behind him. Wanting to be left alone, he turned and stared with annoyance at the elderly man. However, the old man, who turned out to be a Christian, struck up a conversation and learned that Justin was a philosopher. The old man then began to ask some soul-searching questions, helping Justin to see the deficiency of human philosophy. As Justin later reminisced, "When the old man had spoken these and many other things, he left, encouraging me to think about what he had said. I've never seen him since, but immediately a flame was kindled in my soul. I was overwhelmed by a love for the prophets and the friends of Christ. After pondering over the things the old man had said, I realized that Christianity was the only true and worthwhile philosophy."[3]

After becoming a Christian, Justin continued to wear his philosopher's robe to symbolize that he had found the one true philosophy. In fact, he became an evangelist to pagan philosophers and devoted his life to helping educated Romans understand the meaning of Christianity. His written defenses to the Romans are the oldest complete Christian apologies still in existence. Justin proved to be a gifted evangelist, converting many Romans—learned and unlearned alike. In the end, a group of philosophers plotting against his life had him arrested. Choosing to die rather than to denounce Christ, Justin was executed in about 165. After his death, he became known as Justin the Martyr, or simply Justin Martyr.

Clement of Alexandria—Instructor of New Believers

Another philosopher who found Christianity while on a spiritual journey for truth was Clement *(KLEM ent)*. After realizing the inadequacy of human philosophy, he turned to Christianity. After his conversion, he journeyed throughout the Roman Empire, learning the precepts of Christianity firsthand from the oldest, most respected Christian teachers of his age. His writings, which are dated about 190, reflect the composite wisdom of his instructors, and they have inspired many Christians throughout the centuries, including John Wesley.

Clement eventually settled in Alexandria, Egypt. He was made an elder (presbyter) in that congregation and placed in charge of training new Christians. He is generally referred to as "Clement of Alexandria" to distinguish him from another Clement, who was overseer (bishop) of the church of Rome during the last years of the Apostle John. Unless indicated otherwise, references to "Clement" in this book, will mean Clement of Alexandria.

Origen—A Brilliant Mind
Devoted to God

Among Clement's students in Alexandria was a gifted teenager named Origen *(OR ih jen)*, who had been reared in a Christian home. When Origen was 17, a severe persecution broke out in Alexandria, and his father was imprisoned. Origen wrote his father in prison and encouraged him to remain faithful and not to renounce Christ out of fatherly concern for his family. After a date was set for his father's trial, Origen decided to appear at the trial by his father's side and die with him. However, on the night before the trial, while Origen was asleep, his mother hid all of his clothes, preventing him from leaving the house the next morning in time for the trial.

Although he was only 17, Origen distinguished himself in the church of Alexandria by the loving care he gave to his fellow Christians during the fierce persecution raging at the time. The angry mobs noticed his acts of mercy, and he barely survived the persecution with his own life.

Origen had learned grammar and Greek literature from his father, and he began giving private lessons in those subjects to support his younger brothers and sisters. He was so unusually brilliant that many pagan parents sent their sons to be instructed by Origen, and many of these youths became Christians as a result of Origen's witnessing to them.

Meanwhile, Clement, the teacher in charge of training new Christians, had put his life at risk. To the pagan officials he was a marked man. So he was forced to escape to another city to continue his Christian ministry. In an unusual move, the elders of Alexandria appointed Origen, only 18 at the time, to take Clement's place as head of the training school. They chose wisely, and Origen poured his very soul into the task. He quit his short-lived profession as an instructor of grammar and literature, and he sold all of his Greek literary books on credit to another man. He subsisted in poverty off of the small monthly installment payments he received from the sale of his Greek literary books. He refused to accept any payment for his services as a Christian teacher. After teaching new Christian believers all day, he would study the Scriptures far into the night.

Before long, Origen became one of the most respected Christian teachers of his age. Eventually, some of his students asked him to give a series of lectures on the Bible, discussing each book of the Bible, passage by passage. The students paid scribes to take down his words, and these became the first set of Bible commentaries ever written by a Christian. Origen didn't intend for these commentaries to be taken too seriously, since he frequently went off on tangents and personal surmises. Throughout the commentaries, he displayed an amiable, non-dogmatic disposition, frequently ending a discussion by saying, "Well, that's the best I can do with that passage. Maybe someone with more insight has a better explanation." Yet, sometimes in his speculations, Origen expressed some unorthodox views that were not representative of early Christian thought. For that reason, I have been cautious in selecting quotations from him.

Despite his erroneous speculations, Origen possessed one of the most brilliant minds of his day—among Christians and non-Christians alike. He even carried on personal correspondence with one of the Roman emperors. But his fame also attracted the attention of the enemies of Christianity, and several times he was forced to move to new towns in order to escape persecution. Nevertheless, he managed to live until he was 70, when he was finally caught and tortured. No amount of torture could make him deny Jesus, and his tormentors finally gave up in exasperation. However, Origen eventually died from their inhumane treatment.

Tertullian—Apologist to the Romans

To Western Christians, Tertullian (*tur TULL yen*) is perhaps the most familiar of all the early Christian writers. He was a leader in the North African church of Carthage, the place where he eventually settled.[4] Tertullian was one of the most gifted apologists of the early church, and he was one of the few early church elders who wrote in Latin, rather than in Greek. Tertullian is remembered for several memorable sayings, such as "the blood of the martyrs is the seed of the church."

Tertullian penned his writings during a span of about 20 years, from 190 to 210. In addition to his apologetic works, Tertullian wrote several short letters or essays, reassuring Christians in prison and exhorting Christians in general to maintain their separation from the world. He also wrote several defenses of orthodoxy against the heretics of his day.

Later in his life, Tertullian joined the Montanist sect, which was orthodox in theology but which expected its members to follow man-made aesthetic commands. Fortunately, at least half of Tertullian's writings were penned before this sect influenced him. Furthermore, since this group was orthodox in its theology, even the works he wrote after joining the Montanists are generally representative of early Christian thought. Nevertheless, I have been judicious in quoting from any of his Montanistic works.

Cyprian—The Rich Man
Who Gave All to Christ

A few decades after Tertullian penned his works, a wealthy Roman named Cyprian (*SIP ree an*) converted to Christianity at the age of 40. Although he was an admirer of Tertullian, Cyprian never joined the Montanist sect, and he was strongly opposed to any heretical or schismatic groups. As a new Christian, Cyprian was so jubilant to have found Christ and to be born anew that he liquidated his entire estate and gave the money to the poor. He rejoiced to be unfettered from the weight of his material possessions, and his writings contain some of the most moving passages on the Christian rebirth ever penned. The church in Carthage respected his enthusiastic commitment to Christ. Though he had been a Christian only a few years, they selected him to be the overseer (bishop) of their church, a very unusual event in that age.

Cyprian's writings are particularly valuable because they consist chiefly of correspondence with the leaders of other churches, revealing the everyday concerns and problems of Christian congregations in that period. Cyprian was forced to carry on much of his pastoral work underground, since intense persecution raged during much of his ministry. He was a tireless shepherd, pouring out his energy, and ultimately his very life, for the flock that Christ entrusted to him. He was finally arrested by the Romans and beheaded in 258.

Lactantius—Teacher of the
Emperor's Son

Lactantius (*lack TAN she us*) is less familiar to most Christians today. This is our loss, because he wrote with unusual clarity and eloquence. Before embracing Christianity, he had been a celebrated teacher of rhetoric, receiving notice from Emperor

Diocletian. After his conversion, Lactantius dedicated his literary abilities to the cause of Christ. He lived through the last great Roman persecution of Christians in the early 300s, and he eventually settled in France. Although Lactantius was an old man when Constantine became emperor in 312, Constantine asked him to be the personal instructor of his oldest son. The writings of Lactantius are important because they were written at the very end of the pre-Constantine period of the church. They demonstrate that most Christian beliefs had changed very little during the 223 years from the end of the Apostle John's life to the beginning of Constantine's reign.

In Case You've Forgotten Those Names . . .

I can well appreciate that these names are probably unfamiliar to you, and you may have trouble remembering them. For that reason, I've included a Biographical Dictionary at the end of the book. This Dictionary gives a very brief biographical sketch of all the writers I cite in this book. You may want to mark that page with a paper clip or slip of paper, so you can quickly refresh your memory on any of these names as you're reading.

In my early drafts of this book, I merely *described* the early Christians' beliefs and practices, including only one or two actual quotes from the early Christians in each chapter. But the universal comment I received back from friends who reviewed these early chapters was, "We want to hear the *early Christians* talk, not you. Let them tell their story in their own words." So that's what I've done. Here's their story, told largely by them. Hopefully, it will challenge you as much as it did me.

3

Citizens Of
Another Kingdom

Musing over all the things Jesus had done during his brief life on earth, the Apostle John remarked that if they were all put down in writing, "the world itself could not contain the books that would be written" (John 21:25). Yet, on the night before his death, Jesus had to select from all his lessons and teachings a few key points that he particularly wanted his apostles to remember.

He could have talked to them at length about theology. But he didn't. He could have scolded them for all of the mistakes they had made during their time with him. But he didn't. Instead, he chose to review with them the blueprints for the most magnificent building that would ever be constructed in the history of mankind—the church. He graphically demonstrated to the apostles that those who would lead the church must be the servants of all. He also carefully explained what the distinguishing marks of the faithful members of this church would be. Three identifying marks that he stressed were:

1. Separation from the world. "If the world hates you, keep in mind that it hated me first. If you belonged to the world, it would love you as its own. As it is, you do not belong to the world, but I have chosen you out of the world. That is why the world hates you" (John 15:18,19).

2. Unconditional love. "As I have loved you, so you must love one another. By this all men will know that you are my disciples, if you love one another" (John 13:34,35).

3. Obedient trust. "Trust in God; trust also in me.... If anyone loves me, he will obey my teaching" (John 14:1,23).

John recorded those words near the end of the first century. But did the church retain those marks of identification in the century after the apostles? What was the second century church really like?

A People Not Of This World

"No one can serve two masters," declared Jesus to his disciples (Matt. 6:24). However, Christians have spent the greater portion of the past two millenniums apparently trying to prove Jesus wrong. We have told ourselves that we can indeed have both—the things of God and the things of this world. Many of us live our lives no differently than do conservative non-Christians, except for the fact that we attend church regularly each week. We watch the same entertainment. We share the same concerns about the problems of this world. And we are frequently just as involved in the world's commercial and materialistic pursuits. Often, our being "not of this world" exists in theory more than in practice.

But the church was not originally like that. The first Christians lived under a completely different set of principles and values than the rest of mankind. They rejected the world's entertainment, honors, and riches. They were already citizens of another kingdom, and they listened to the voice of a different Master. This was as true of the second century church as it was of the first.

The work of an unknown author, written in about 130, describes Christians to the Romans as follows: "They dwell in their own countries simply as sojourners.... They are in the flesh, but they do not live after the flesh. They pass their days on earth, but they are citizens of heaven. They obey the prescribed laws, and at the same time, they surpass the laws by their lives. They love all men but are persecuted by all. They are unknown and condemned. They are put to death, but [will be] restored to life. They are poor, yet they make many rich. They possess few things; yet, they abound in all. They are dishonored, but in their very dishonor are glorified.... And those who hate them are unable to give any reason for their hatred."[1]

Because the earth wasn't their home, the early Christians could say without reservation, like Paul, "to live is Christ, and to die is gain" (Phil. 1:21). Justin Martyr explained to the Romans, "Since our thoughts are not fixed on the present, we are not concerned when men put us to death. Death is a debt we must all pay anyway."[2]

A second-century elder exhorted his congregation, "Brothers, let us willingly leave our sojourn in this present world so we can do the will of Him who called us. And let us not fear to depart out of this world,... deeming the things of this world as not belonging to us, and not fixing our desires upon them.... The Lord declares, 'No servant can serve two masters.' If we desire, then, to serve both God and Money, it will be unprofitable for us. 'For what will it profit if a man gains the whole world, and loses his own soul?' This world and the next are two enemies.... We cannot therefore be the friends of both."[3]

Cyprian, the respected overseer of the church in Carthage, stressed a similar theme in a letter he wrote to a Christian friend: "The one peaceful and trustworthy tranquility, the one security that is solid, firm, and never changing, is this: for a man to withdraw from the distractions of this world, anchor himself to the firm ground of salvation, and lift his eyes from earth to heaven.... He who is actually greater than the world can crave nothing, can desire nothing, from this world. How stable, how unshakable is that safeguard, how heavenly is the protection in its never-ending blessings—to be free from the snares of this entangling world, to be purged from the dregs of earth, and fitted for the light of eternal immortality."[4]

The same themes run throughout all the writings of the early Christians, from Europe to North Africa: we can't have both Christ and the world.

Lest we think that the early Christians were describing a lifestyle they didn't really practice, we have the testimony of the Romans themselves. One pagan antagonist of the Christians remarked:

□ □ □ □ □ □ □ □ □ □

They despise the temples as houses of the dead. They reject the gods. They laugh at sacred things. Wretched, they pity our priests. Half-naked themselves, they despise honors and purple robes. What incredible audacity and foolishness! They are not afraid of present torments, but they fear those that are uncertain and future. While they do not fear to die for the present, they fear to die after death....

At least learn from your present situation, you wretched people, what actually awaits you after death. See, many of you—in fact, by your own admission, the majority of you—are in want, are cold, are hungry, and are laboring in hard work. Yet, your god allows it. He is either unwilling or unable to assist his people. So he is either weak or unjust.... Take notice! For you there are threats, punishments, tortures, and crosses.... Where is the god who is supposed to help you when you come back from the dead? He cannot even help you in this life! Do not the Romans, without any help from your god, govern, rule over, and have the enjoyment of the whole world, including dominion over you yourselves?

In the meantime, living in suspense and anxiety, you abstain from respectable pleasures. You do not attend sporting events. You have no interest in public amusements. You reject the public banquets, and abhor the sacred games.... Thus, wretched as you are, you will neither rise from the dead, nor enjoy life in the meanwhile. So, if you have any wisdom or sense, stop prying into the heavens and the destinies and secrets of the world.... Persons who are unable to understand civil matters are certainly unable to discuss divine ones.[5]

□ □ □ □ □ □ □ □ □ □

When I first read the criticisms that the Romans leveled against the Christians, I painfully realized that no one would accuse Christians today of those same charges. We aren't criticized for being totally absorbed in the interests of a heavenly kingdom, ignoring the things the world has to offer. In fact, Christians today are accused of just the opposite—of being money hungry and hypocritical in our devotion to God.

A Love Without Condition

At no other time in the history of Christianity did love so characterize the entire church as it did in the first three centuries. And Roman society took note. Tertullian reported that the Romans would exclaim, "See how they love one another!"[6]

Justin Martyr sketched Christian love this way: "We who used to value the acquisition of wealth and possessions more than anything else now bring what we have into a common fund and share it with anyone who needs it. We used to hate and destroy one another and refused to associate with people of another race or country. Now, because of Christ, we live together with such people and pray for our enemies."[7]

Clement, describing the person who has come to know God, wrote, "He impoverishes himself out of love, so that he is certain he may never overlook a brother in need, especially if he knows he can bear poverty better than his brother. He likewise considers the pain of another as his own pain. And if he suffers any hardship because of having given out of his own poverty, he does not complain."[8]

When a devastating plague swept across the ancient world in the third century, Christians were the only ones who cared for the sick, which they did at the risk of contracting the plague themselves. Meanwhile, pagans were throwing infected members of their own families into the streets even before they died, in order to protect themselves from the disease.[9]

Another example illustrates both the brotherly love of Christians and their uncompromising commitment to Jesus as Lord. A pagan actor became a Christian, but he realized he had to change his employment because most plays encouraged immorality and were steeped in pagan idolatry. Furthermore, the theater sometimes purposefully turned boys into homosexuals so they could better play the roles of women on stage. Since this newly-converted actor had no other job skills, he considered establishing an acting school to teach drama to non-Christian students. However, he first submitted his idea to the leaders of his church for their counsel.

The leaders told him that if acting was an immoral profession then it would be wrong to train others in it. Nevertheless, since this was a rather novel question, they wrote to Cyprian in nearby Carthage for his thoughts. Cyprian agreed that a profession unfit for a Christian to practice was also unfit for him to teach, even if this was his sole means of support.

How many of us would be so concerned about righteousness that we would submit our employment decisions to our body of elders or board of deacons? How many church leaders today would be so concerned about offending God that they would take such an uncompromising position?

But that isn't the end of the story. Cyprian also told this neighboring church that they should be willing to support the actor if he had no other means of earning a living—just as they supported orphans, widows, and other needy persons. Going further, he wrote, "If your church is financially unable to support him, he may move over to us and here receive whatever he needs for food and clothing."[10] Cyprian and his church didn't even know this actor, yet they were willing to support him because he was a fellow believer. As one Christian told the Romans, "We love one another with a mutual love because we do not know how to hate."[11] If Christians today made such a statement to the world, would the world believe it?

The love of the early Christians wasn't limited simply to their fellow believers. Christians also lovingly helped nonbelievers: the poor, the orphans, the elderly, the sick, the shipwrecked—even their persecutors.[12] Jesus had said, "Love your enemies and pray for those who persecute you" (Matt. 5:44). The early Christians accepted this statement as a command from their Lord, rather than as an ideal that couldn't be actually practiced in real life.

Lactantius wrote, "If we all derive our origin from one man, whom God created, we are plainly all of one family. Therefore it must be considered an abomination to hate another human, no matter how guilty he may be. For this reason, God has decreed that we should hate no one, but that we should eliminate hatred. So we can comfort our enemies by reminding them of our mutual relationship. For if we have all been given life from the same God, what else are we but brothers? ... Because we are all brothers, God teaches us to never do evil to one another, but only good—giving aid to those who are oppressed and experiencing hardship, and giving food to the hungry."[13]

The Scriptures teach that a Christian shouldn't take his brother to court. Rather, he should suffer fraud at the hands of his brother, if need be. (1 Cor. 6:7) However, as an attorney, I've seen that Christians today don't hesitate to sue their brothers and sisters in Christ. A particularly disturbing case happened recently in the town where I live. A student at a local Christian school worked on campus in his spare time to help pay his tuition. One day he was overcome from the fumes of some insecticide he was spraying in the school building, and he was briefly hospitalized. The school's method of applying the insecticide was apparently improper. The result? The parents sued the Christian school for more than half a million dollars. In contrast, early Christians not only refused to take their fellow Christians to court, most of them refused to take *anyone* to court, since they viewed every human as their brother or sister.

It's no wonder that Christianity spread rapidly throughout the ancient world, even though there were few organized missionary or evangelism programs. The love they practiced drew the attention of the world, just as Jesus said it would.

A Childlike Trust In God

To the early Christian, trusting God meant more than a teary-eyed testimony about "the time I came to trust the Lord." It meant believing that even if obedience to God entailed great suffering, God was trustworthy to bring a person through it.

"A person who does not do what God has commanded shows he really does not believe God,"[14] Clement declared. To the early Christians, to claim to trust God while refusing to obey Him was a contradiction (1 John 2:4). Their Christianity was more than verbal. As one early Christian expressed it, "We don't speak great things—we live them!"[15]

One distinguishing mark of the early Christians was their childlike, literal obedience to the teachings of Jesus and the apostles. They didn't feel they had to understand the reason for a commandment before they would obey it. They just trusted that God's way was always the best way. Clement asked, "Who then is so irreverent as to disbelieve God, and to demand explanations from God as from men?"[16]

They trusted God because they lived in awe of His majesty and wisdom. Felix, a Christian lawyer in Rome and a contemporary of Tertullian, put it this way: "God is greater than all our perceptions—He is infinite, immense. Only He truly understands His true greatness; our hearts are too limited to really understand Him. We are making a worthy estimation of Him when we say that He is beyond estimation.... Anyone who thinks he knows the magnitude of God, diminishes His greatness."[17]

The supreme example of their absolute trust in God was their acceptance of persecution. From the time of the Emperor Trajan (around A.D. 100) until the Edict of Milan was issued in 313, the practice of Christianity was illegal within the boundaries of the Roman Empire. Being a Christian was a crime punishable by death. But the Roman officials didn't generally hunt out Christians. They ignored them unless someone formally accused a person of being a Christian. As a result, persecution was intermittent. Christians in one town would suffer horrible tortures and death while Christians in a nearby area would be untouched. It was totally unpredictable. Yet, every Christian lived daily with a death sentence hanging over his head.

The very fact that Christians were willing to suffer unspeakable horrors and to die rather than disown their God was, next to their lifestyle, their single most effective evangelistic tool. Few, if any, Romans would die for their gods. There had to be some substance to Christianity if it meant so much to those who practiced it. In fact, the Greek word for "witness" is martyr. Not surprisingly, this is also the Greek word for "martyr." In many places where our Bibles use the word "witness," the early Christians were reading "martyr." For example, in our Bibles, Revelation 2:13 refers to "Antipas, my faithful witness, who was put to death in your city." The early Christians were understanding the passage to say, "Antipas, my faithful martyr." Although most Christians tried to flee local persecution when possible, they rejected any mass exodus from the Roman Empire. Like little children, they believed their Master when He said His Church would be built on a rock and that the gates of Hades could not overpower it (Matt. 16:18).

They realized that thousands of them might die monstrous deaths, experience excruciating tortures, and suffer imprisonment. But they were absolutely convinced that their Father wouldn't let the church be annihilated. Christians stood before the Romans with naked hands, letting them know that Christians would not use human means to try to preserve the church. They trusted God, and God alone, as their protector.

As Origen told the Romans: "When God gives the Tempter permission to persecute us, we suffer persecution. And when God wishes us to be free from suffering, even though surrounded by a world that hates us, we enjoy a wonderful peace. We trust in the protection of the One who said, 'Be of good cheer, for I have overcome the world.' And truly He has overcome the world. Therefore, the world prevails only as long as it is permitted to by Him who received power from the Father to overcome the world. From His victory we take courage. Even if He should again wish us to suffer and contend for our faith, let the enemy come against us. We will say to them, 'I can do all things through Christ Jesus our Lord who strengthens me.'"[18]

Origen had lost his father to persecution when he was a teenager, and he himself eventually died from torture and imprisonment at the hands of the Romans. Yet, with unshakable confidence he told the Romans, "Eventually, every form of worship will be destroyed except the religion of Christ, which alone will stand. In fact, it will one day triumph, for its teachings take hold of men's minds more and more each day."[19]

4

Is Right And Wrong Simply A Matter Of Culture?

Early Christianity was a revolution that swept through the ancient world like fire through dry timber. It was a countercultural movement that challenged the pivotal institutions of Roman society. As Tertullian wrote: "Our contest lies against the institutions of our ancestors, against the authority of tradition, against man-made laws, against the reasonings of the worldly wise, against antiquity, and against customs."[1]

How strange it is, therefore, that the modern church claims that the Christians of the first few centuries were merely teaching and practicing the culture of their day. This is particularly ironic since the Romans bitterly criticized the Christians for just the opposite—for not following the cultural norms of their day.

But the relationship of the early Christians to their culture is not simply a matter of past history. It is something that should deeply concern the church today. For most of the cultural issues facing twentieth-century Christians are the very same issues that faced the early church. However, our response to these issues has generally been quite different than theirs.

Divorce—A Roman Plague

As in most societies, the family was the core unit of Roman civilization. But as is true today, marriages were often unhappy. Both husbands and wives frequently had lovers. By the time of Christ, extramarital affairs on the part of both husbands and wives were so frequent that they were no longer scandalous.

Not surprisingly, divorce was fairly commonplace. Roman men and women often married four or five times. As Tertullian remarked, "As for divorce, women long for it as though it were the natural consequence of marriage."[2] In Roman society, most marriages were arranged by the parents of the bride and groom. Newly wedded couples were not usually in love with each other and often hardly knew each other on their wedding day. Frequently, there was a considerable age difference between husband and wife. This was true among Christians as well as Roman society in general. So it would be far easier to justify divorce in Roman society than in twentieth century America.

Nevertheless, the early Christians didn't rationalize matters from a human viewpoint. Even though divorce was considered perfectly proper in their society, they didn't permit divorce except for adultery.[3] As Origen wrote, "'What God has joined together, let no man separate'—neither government nor any other power. For God, who joined them together, is more mighty than all others that a person could name or even conceive."[4] Christians took Jesus' words seriously when He said, "Anyone who divorces his wife, except for marital unfaithfulness, and marries another woman commits adultery" (Matt. 19:9).[5]

The strict position of the early Christians against divorce obviously wasn't a reflection of their culture. But what about *our* attitude toward divorce? Haven't our views followed the trends of our culture? Forty years ago, an evangelical Christian wouldn't have dreamed of divorcing his or her spouse merely because of "incompatibility." Today, the divorce rate among evangelicals is fast approaching that of the world.[6] What has changed? Certainly not Scripture. Rather, the conservative bloc of American society has changed its views on divorce. Evangelicals often pride themselves for opposing "worldly" attitudes and trends. But in reality, what we so often oppose is merely the liberal segment of the world. Once a practice is accepted by the conservative element, the church soon follows in stride. Divorce is a prime example.

Abortion—Not A 20th Century Phenomenon

As is true of the world today, Romans were concerned about unwanted pregnancies. Lacking the modern means of birth control, Romans took care of unwanted pregnancies in three ways: strangling newborn babies, abandoning babies by the roadside (where they either died or were taken as slaves), or aborting the fetus. Contrary to what you may have thought, abortion is no twentieth century invention. The Christian lawyer Mark Felix chided the Romans, "There are some women among you who by drinking special potions extinguish the life of the future human in their very bowels, thus committing murder before they even give birth."[7]

Again, the early Christians took a strong stand against what was considered a completely moral, civilized practice. When some Romans raised the ridiculous charge against Christians that they murdered and ate infants as part of their religious ceremonies, Athenagoras, a Christian apologist who wrote around 170 A.D., answered those charges with these words: "When we say that those women who use drugs to bring on abortion actually commit murder and will have to render an account to God for this, how could we possibly murder [infants]? It would not make sense for us to regard the very fetus in the womb as a created being, and therefore an object of God's care, and then when it is born to kill it."[8]

Tertullian explained to the Romans, "In our case, since murder is absolutely forbidden in any form, we may not destroy even the fetus in the womb.... To hinder a birth is merely a speedier form of killing. It matters not whether you take away a life that is born, or destroy one that has not yet come to birth."[9]

Admirably, evangelical Christians today have generally stood just as uncompromisingly against abortion as the early Christians did. I hope that our stance is completely independent of our culture, but I don't know that it is. The conservative bloc of American society hasn't yet accepted abortion; conservative lawmakers and justices are normally opposed to it. If their attitudes change, will ours follow suit? Right now it seems impossible that we would ever change our attitudes on abortion. However, a century ago, nobody dreamed that divorce would someday be commonplace in the evangelical church.

High Fashion And Low Modesty

Peter had instructed women, "Your beauty should not come from outward adornment, such as braided hair and the wearing of gold jewelry and fine clothes" (1 Pet. 3:3). Paul gave similar instructions: "I also want women to dress modestly, with decency and propriety, not with braided hair or gold or pearls or expensive clothes, but with good deeds, appropriate for women who profess to worship God" (1 Tim. 2:9,10). In giving these exhortations, the apostles weren't simply reinforcing the cultural norms of their day. They were doing just the opposite.

A fashionable Roman woman used virtually every beauty aid that her modern day counterpart uses. She began the day by arranging her hair and putting on her make-up. She painted her lips, applied black eye shadow, put on false eye lashes, coated her face with white powder, and smoothed rouge onto her cheeks. She wore her hair in an elaborate hairdo, complete with curls, bangs, and ornate layers of braids. Some women wore imported wigs from India, and many dyed their hair blond.

One Roman commented to his female friend, "While you remain at home,... your hair is at the hairdresser's, you take out your teeth at night, and you sleep tucked away in a hundred cosmetics boxes. Even your face does not sleep with you! Then you wink at men under an eyebrow you took out of a drawer that same morning."[10]

Roman women adorned the rest of their bodies as much as their faces. When going out, they would array themselves with jewels, often wearing expensive rings on every finger. Fashionable women insisted on wearing gowns made of imported materials such as silk, even though, pound for pound, silk cost as much as gold. Clement commented whimsically, "The body of such ladies wouldn't fetch a thousand drachmas [a coin of little value], but they will pay ten thousand talents [more than the average Roman earned in a lifetime] for a single dress. So their clothes are worth more than they are."[11] Even many Roman men wore cosmetics and dressed as lavishly as the women.

In contrast, the church discouraged the use of cosmetics and exhorted men and women to be content with simple clothing. Not only was simple clothing less costly, but luxurious dresses were often transparent and clung sensuously to a woman's figure. Clement remarked, "Luxurious clothing that cannot conceal the shape of the body is no covering at all. Such clothing, clinging close to the body, takes the body's shape and adheres to the flesh. It outlines the woman's figure, so that the whole shape of her body is visible to spectators, even though they cannot actually see the body itself.... Such clothing is meant for looking, not for covering."[12]

Nevertheless, the early church did not try to legislate the type of clothing Christians should wear. While the church emphasized the principles of simple, modest dress, the specific application of those principles was left up to the individual Christian.

Aside from clothing, the Christian's standard of modesty, for both men and women, also differed from those of Roman society. This was particularly apparent in public and private baths. Few other societies, except for the Japanese, have had such a penchant for hot baths. Bathing was the national pastime, and public baths were one of the primary meeting places of Roman society. In the early days of the Roman Republic, baths for men and women had been strictly segregated. However, by the second century, mixed bathing in the nude was customary.[13]

Upper class Romans often had baths in their homes, but modesty there was little different. Clement describes these private baths: "Some women will scarcely undress in front of their own husbands out of a pretense of modesty. But anyone else who wants to may see them at home shut up naked in their baths. For they are not embarrassed to strip before spectators, as if exposing their bodies for sale.... Those who have not become utterly destitute of modesty shut out strangers, yet they bathe with their own servants. They even strip naked in front of their slaves and are massaged by them."[14]

In sharp contrast, Christians taught that men and women should not bathe publicly in each other's presence. Their attitudes toward modesty weren't a reflection of Roman culture, but of godly culture.[15]

Don't the Roman attitudes on modesty also have their parallels in today's American society? Most Americans would be quite embarrassed to be seen in public in their underwear. Yet, they think nothing of relaxing at a poolside in swimsuits that are no less revealing. And don't we Christians generally follow right along with our culture? We appear in public in swimwear that would have shocked even non-Christians only 50 years ago. Yet because our swimwear is acceptable to the modern conservative community, we think nothing of it. I say this in self-criticism because I used to label Christians who objected to modern swimsuits as being prudish or Victorian. The testimony of the early Christians has made me re-think my position.

Roman R-Rated Entertainment

Upper class Romans enjoyed a lot of leisure time. They filled their evenings and holidays with gluttonous banquets, the theater, and sporting events at the arena. Banquets sometimes lasted as long as ten hours. It was not unheard of for a banquet to consist of twenty-two courses, including such delicacies as pig's udders and peacock tongues. But Christians took no delight in these gluttonous feasts.

The Roman theater was borrowed from the Greeks, and the favorite dramatic themes were crime, adultery and immorality. Either boys or prostitutes played the female roles. Although the theater was a favorite pastime of educated Romans, Christians shunned the theater with disgust. Lactantius wrote, "I am inclined to think that the corrupting influence of the stage is even worse [than that of the arena]. The subjects of comedies are the deflowering of virgins or the loves of prostitutes.... Similarly, the tragedies parade before the eyes [of the audience] the murder of parents and acts of incest committed by wicked kings.... Is the art of the mimes any better? They teach adultery by acting it out. How do we expect our young people to respond when they see that these things are practiced without shame and that everyone eagerly watches."[16]

Tertullian added, "The father who carefully protects and guards his virgin daughter's ears from every polluting word takes her to the theater himself, exposing her to all its vile language and attitudes." He asked rhetorically, "How can it be right to *look* at the things that are wrong to *do*? How can those things which defile a man when they go out of his mouth not defile him when going in through his eyes and ears?"[17] (Matt. 15:17-20).

Although it was mainly the upper class Romans who attended the theater and banquets, the rich and poor alike enjoyed the arena. The games in the arena were designed to quench the Romans' undying thirst for violence, brutality, and blood. The brutal chariot races were the favorite event. In the course of these races, chariots would inevitably crash, catapulting their drivers onto the racetrack, where they would either be dragged to death by the panic-stricken horses or trampled by another driver's team. All the while, the crowd would go wild with excitement.

However, the death and violence that accompanied chariot racing failed to satisfy the Roman thirst for blood. So wild animals, sometimes hundreds of them, were brought into the arena to fight each other—wolves against stags, lions against bulls, packs of dogs against bears—and just about any other combination that twisted minds could dream of. Sometimes armed men hunted down animals; other times, starved animals hunted down unarmed Christians. But the Romans wanted even more. So human gladiators were pitted against each other to fight to the death. Gladiators were normally prisoners who had already been condemned to death. The Romans thought they were being noble to give these men a "fighting chance." If a gladiator triumphed in repeated fights, he could eventually win his freedom. Once again, however, Christians didn't follow the culture of their day. Lactantius told his fellow Romans:

> He who finds it pleasurable to watch a man being killed, even though the man has been legally con-demned, pollutes his conscience just as much as though he were an accomplice or willing spectator of a murder committed in secret. Yet they call these 'sports'—where human blood is shed! ... When they see men placed under the stroke of death, begging for mercy, can they be righteous

when they not only permit the men to be killed, but *demand* it? They cast their cruel and inhuman votes for death, not being satisfied by the mere flowing of blood or the presence of gashing wounds. In fact, they *order* the [gladiators]—although wounded and lying on the ground—to be attacked again and their corpses to be pummeled with blows, to make certain they are not merely feigning death.

The crowds are even angry with the gladiators if one of the two isn't slain quickly. As though they thirsted for human blood, they hate delays.... By steeping themselves in this practice, they have lost their humanity.... Therefore, it is not fitting that we who strive to stay on the path of righteousness should share in this public homicide. When God forbids us to kill, he not only prohibits the violence that is condemned by public laws, but he also forbids the violence that is deemed lawful by men.[18]

Are we willing to take such an uncompromising stand toward entertainment today? After reading such counsel, I stepped back and took a look at myself. I had to admit that I had been letting my culture dictate my standards for entertainment. Yes, I avoided movies that would be considered risque by the conservative community. Nevertheless, I still ended up watching entertainment that was saturated with violence, crime, and immorality. I was willing to accept obscenity, profanity and flashes of nudity—so long as the motion picture industry didn't give the movie a rating worse than PG-13. So I had let the motion picture industry decide for me what was and wasn't fit to see. My culture had determined my standards for entertainment.

Evolution Before Darwin

The Romans could enjoy watching other humans being slaughtered with swords and torn apart by wild animals because they believed that man was simply a highly developed animal. The belief that humans have slowly evolved into their present form of life isn't a modern view at all. And the belief that the universe came into being because of the chance collision of particles of matter isn't new either. Educated Romans shared many of the same views as today's secular scientists.

One early Christian wrote, "Some men deny the existence of any Divine power. Others inquire daily as to whether or not one exists. Still others would construct the whole fabric of the universe by chance accidents and by random collision, fashioning it by the movement of atoms of different shapes."[19] Yes, even the term "atom" isn't a twentieth century invention, but a term coined by Greek philosophers.

Lactantius also discussed the Roman scientific thought of his day: "Some people teach that the first men lived nomadic lives among the woods and plains. They were not united by any bond of speech or laws. Instead, they lived in caves and grottos, using leaves and grass for their beds. They were prey to the beasts and stronger animals. Eventually, those who had escaped, having been torn [by wild beasts] ... sought out the company of other men for protection. At first they communicated to each other by nods; then they tried elementary forms of speech. By attaching names to various objects, they little by little developed a system of speech."[20]

The Christian belief that all humans can trace their origin to the first human pair meant that all humans were equally brothers and sisters—a rather novel idea to Roman culture. So by teaching divine creation, Christians weren't simply parroting what everybody else in their culture already believed. In fact, educated Greeks and Romans ridiculed Christians for their belief in creation. Those same intellectuals freely accepted the writings of other ethnic groups concerning the origin of man—no matter how ridiculous they were. But they summarily rejected the writings of Jews and Christians on the subject of creation—no matter how much sense they made.[21]

To The Romans, All Persons Were *Not* Created Equal

Virtually every human society has maintained class distinctions, and Rome was no exception. Wealthy Romans looked down on poor Romans. Freemen looked down on slaves. Certain occupations were viewed as superior to others. Even the Jews had such class distinctions among themselves. Roman citizens viewed themselves as superior to all other peoples. Once again, however, the early Christians went against the cultural current of the day. In fact, their teachings on the brotherhood of man were nothing short of revolutionary.

Clement wrote, "[God] gave His own Son to all persons in common, and He created all things for everyone. Therefore, all things are common to all and are not for the rich to appropriate an undue share. The expression, 'I possess, and possess in abundance, so why should I not enjoy?' is suitable neither for the individual nor for society. More worthy of love is: 'I have; so why shouldn't I give to those who need.'... It is monstrous for one person to live in luxury, while many are in want."[22]

Writing a century later, Lactantius stated:

> In God's sight, no one is a slave; no one is a master. Since we all have the same Father, we are all equally His children. No one is poor in God's sight except the one lacking in justice. No one is rich except the one with an abundance of virtues.... The reason why neither the Romans nor the Greeks could possess justice was that they had so many class distinctions. The rich and the poor. The

powerful and the lowly. The highest authority of kings, and the common individual.... However, someone may say, "Isn't it true that among Christians some are poor and others are rich? Some are masters and others are servants? Isn't there some distinction between persons?" But there is none. In fact, the very reason we call each other brothers is that we believe we are all equal.... Although the physical circumstances of Christian lives may differ, we view no persons as servants. Instead, we speak of them—and treat them—as brothers in spirit and as fellow-servants of Christ.[23]

The Role Of Women In Roman Religion

Paul had told the Corinthians, "Women should remain silent in the churches. They are not allowed to speak, but must be in submission, as the Law says.... for it is disgraceful for a woman to speak in the church." (1 Cor. 14:34,35) And he told Timothy, "A woman should learn in quietness and full submission. I do not permit a woman to teach or to have authority over a man; she must be silent" (1 Tim. 2:11,12).

In no other area are the Scriptures so frequently attacked today than on this teaching about the role of women in the church. It's frequently said that the apostles and early Christians were simply reinforcing the cultural attitudes of their time concerning the role of women in religion and society. But Roman women were hardly known for their submissive character. As one Roman commented, "We rule the world, but our women rule us."[24]

In Roman religions, women served in the same roles as men. Female high priestesses governed many temples. Mark Felix, a Christian lawyer, described Roman religion this way: "There is a certain place where a man may not go. Others are restricted from women. It is a crime for a slave even to be present at some religious ceremonies. Some temples are governed by a woman with one husband, and others by a woman with many husbands."[25] In fact, the leading religious figure in the ancient Mediterranean world was the oracle (or prophetess) of Delphi. And this oracle was always a woman.

If the role of women in the church had been simply a matter of culture, and not apostolic teaching, we would expect to find that women served the same roles in both the orthodox church and the heretical groups. But this isn't the case. Women were allowed to teach and officiate in most heretical sects. Tertullian made this comment about the role of women in such groups, "They are bold enough to teach, to dispute, to enact exorcisms, to undertake healings, and perhaps even to baptize."[26] The two leading figures in the Montanist sect (after the death of its founder, Montanus) were both women: Maximilla and Priscilla. In fact most of the prophecies and new teachings in this sect came from its female members.

So the exclusion of women from roles of teaching and oversight in the church was definitely not a matter of following Roman culture.

"Wait a minute," you may be thinking. "Maybe the church didn't follow Roman culture in this matter, but it certainly was following *Jewish* culture." And it's true that women were excluded from the Jewish priesthood. But remember that the Jewish priesthood wasn't a product of human culture. It was divinely instituted. Furthermore, by the middle of the second century, the vast majority of Christians were Gentiles, and they most definitely didn't follow Jewish culture. They didn't keep the Sabbath, practice circumcision, follow Jewish dietary laws, observe Jewish festivals, or follow any other Jewish customs that didn't specifically coincide with Christian teaching.

The early church simply obeyed the apostolic teachings on the role of women in the church, the same as they obeyed all the other teachings of the apostles. And once again, they went *against* Roman culture, rather than following it.

Feminists and modern theologians claim that the church's position on women was a product of the contempt for women held by the apostles and early church leaders. But the writings of the early Christians speak differently. For example, Felix wrote, "Let everyone know that all humans are born alike, with a capacity and ability to reason and to feel, without preference of age, sex, or dignity."[27] Clement wrote, "Let us ... understand that the virtue of man and woman is the same. For if the God of both is one, the master of both is also one."[28]

But let's come back to us. Why is it that the role of women in the church has become such an issue today? Is it because we've found new Bible manuscripts that teach differently than our present Bibles? Or is it because our *culture* says that men and women should not perform different roles? Once again, who is unable to resist the culture of the day—we or the early Christians?

Is Conservative
The Same As Godly?

Christians today frequently pride themselves on being different from the world, but in reality they are usually only different from *a particular segment* of the world.

Liberal Christians think they are different from the world because they do not share the bigotry, provincialism, and narrow-mindedness that sometimes characterizes the conservative bloc of our society. But in truth the attitudes and lifestyle of liberal Christians are little different from that of liberal non-Christians.

The same principle is true of evangelicals. Because we cling to conservative American values, we tell ourselves that we're acting independently of our culture. But conservative attitudes can be just as much a part of the world as liberal ones. Haven't our attitudes on divorce, entertainment, and other issues changed in response to changes in our culture?

In fact, there is little difference spiritually between molding ourselves after the liberal segment of society or molding ourselves after the conservative segment of society. The reason is that what's considered conservative today was liberal only a few decades ago.

I still remember a conversation I had in 1969 with a disc jockey who was in his mid-thirties. We had a lively discussion about the issues that were prominent at the time—racial discrimination, police brutality, drugs and the Vietnam war. From the nature of his radio program, I was rather taken aback by his staunchly conservative views, so I finally remarked, "You're really a hard-line right-winger, aren't you!"

He smiled and then replied, "No, I'm not even conservative. I'm actually middle-of-the-road." He paused for a moment, studying my skeptical face. Then with a grin he added, "It's just that the road has moved."

At the time, I dismissed his words as a self-serving rationalization. But his remark stuck with me. I've come to see exactly how right he was. The road is still moving. We're only fooling ourselves when we equate conservative attitudes with godly attitudes.

In reality, the twentieth century church is married to the world. The attitudes, lifestyle, and issues of the world are soon the attitudes, lifestyle, and issues of the church. Russ Taff, a popular Christian singer, recently made this candid observation about today's evangelical church: "Christians go to counselors, Christians have family problems, and Christians become alcoholics. The only difference between believers and non-believers is our simple faith in our Creator God, who loves us and helps us every day." I think Russ Taff's analysis is an honest one. But I also think it's very sad that this is all we Christians today can truthfully say.

Originally, Christians were very different from the society they lived in. Their lifestyle was their primary means of witnessing. Of course, not everyone lived the godly life I have described in this chapter. Still, the lifestyle I have described was the *normal* Christian lifestyle of the early centuries.

So why were *they* able to live independently of their culture, when *we* find it so difficult to do so? What power did they have that we're lacking?

5

Why They Succeeded Where We Often Fail

Years ago, when I began my study of early Christian writings, I was primarily interested in tracing the historical development of Christian doctrine. It was an academic challenge. I wasn't expecting to be inspired or challenged by what I read. But it didn't work out that way. I was soon deeply moved by the testimony and lifestyle of the early Christians. "So this is what absolute surrender means," I said to myself. Although I'm often viewed as a Christian of above-average commitment in my Christian circles, I painfully realized that in the early church I would be considered a compromising, spiritually weak member.

The more I read, the more I longed to have the close walk with God that the early Christians enjoyed. I wanted so much to be able to shrug off the cares of this world as they had. I wanted to pattern my life and attitudes solely after Christ—not after 20th century culture. But I seemed so powerless to do so. Why could they do what I couldn't? I began searching for answers in their writings, where I found three primary reasons:

- **the supportive role of the church;**
- **the message of the cross;**
- **the belief that obedience was a joint venture between man and God.**

41

How The Church Helped
Individuals To Grow Spiritually

"No man is an island,"[1] wrote the sixteenth century Christian poet, John Donne. Humans are by nature social creatures, and we tend to conform to the society around us. That's why it's so hard to swim against the current of our culture. Yet there have been times in human society when large numbers of people have rejected the values and lifestyle of their culture. The hippie movement of the '60s is a prime example. During the '60s, thousands of young people—many of whom were from middle class backgrounds—rejected the materialistic pursuits and the fashionable dress of mainstream America. Instead, they pursued a different way of life.

What enabled those young people to break out of their cultural mold and be non-conformists? The answer lies in the fact that they weren't really non-conformists. They just conformed to a different society.

This was one of the secrets of the early Christians. They were able to reject the ungodly attitudes, practices, and entertainment of their culture because they had conformed to a different culture. Tens of thousands of other Christians shared the same values, attitudes, and standards of entertainment. All the individual Christian had to do was *conform*—conform to the body of believers. Without the church, practicing a godly lifestyle would have been infinitely more difficult.

Cyprian observed, "Break a branch from a tree, and when broken it will not be able to bud. Cut off a stream of water from its source, and it will soon dry up."[2]

The early church was a disciplined church. Yet unlike some later religious groups, the early Christians generally didn't try to legislate righteousness through a plethora of rules and regulations. Instead, they relied on sound teaching, righteous example, and voluntary commitment. Churches that depend on extensive rules to produce personal holiness usually end up producing Pharisees instead. For this reason, the early church emphasized the need for new believers to change *from the inside out*. Externals were considered worthless unless they reflected what was happening inside a person.

Clement explained, "God does not crown those who abstain from wickedness by compulsion, but those who abstain by choice. It is impossible for a person to consistently live righteously except by his own choice. The one who is made 'righteous' by the compulsion of another is not truly righteous.... It is the freedom of each person that produces true righteousness and reveals true wickedness."[3]

For example, despite its teachings about simple dress, the early church didn't require individual Christians to wear any special or distinctive type of clothing, and early Christians didn't all dress alike. Even though the church opposed cosmetics, some Christian women used them anyway. Other Christians ignored the counsel of the church and attended the theater and the arena. And they were not put out of the church for doing so. Nevertheless, the church's method was effective, for even the Romans testified to the fact that most Christians voluntarily followed the direction of the church in these matters.[4]

Of course, the church can effectively teach by example only if it, as a body, has conformed to the teachings of Christ. Otherwise, the church can be as much a hindrance as a help. For example, what would be the attitude of most Christians today toward a believer who dressed simply and modestly, regardless of fashion? Who took no interest in the violent sports of today? Who refused to watch television programs and movies that centered on immorality or that were spiced with profanity and graphic violence? Let's be honest—he would probably be viewed as a fanatic!

Moreover, if a *whole group* of Christians lived that way, they would probably be called a cult. In short, the twentieth-century *church* would view such Christians in the same way that the *Romans* viewed the early Christians. For a present-day Christian to live like the early Christians, he would truly have to be a non-conformist. And it's extremely difficult to be a non-conformist.

Shepherds Who Graduated From The School Of Hard Knocks

The church-wide commitment of the early Christians was a direct reflection of the quality of their leadership.

Today's evangelical churches are typically governed by a pastor and a body of elders and/or a board of deacons. Normally, the pastor is a professionally-trained man with a seminary degree who wasn't raised in the congregation that has hired him. Frequently, he has no governing authority in the congregation other than the power of persuasion. The body of elders or board of deacons are normally men with full-time secular jobs. They oversee church finances and programs, and they often establish church policy. But typically, no one in the church goes to them for spiritual counseling, and they aren't usually the shepherds of the flock.

Although we use many of the same names for church leaders as did the early Christians—such as elders (or presbyters) and deacons—our church government differs considerably from theirs in *substance*. Instead of a sole professional pastor, the entire body of elders (presbyters) were full-time pastors in the early churches. As Christianity grew, all Christians in a given city were not able to meet together in one place. But each separate fellowship of believers in that city had at least one elder or presbyter to shepherd them. And each city had one overseer or bishop who exercised oversight over all of the individual congregations in that city. This helped to unify the local bodies of believers. As a result, the early Christians could truly speak of the *church* in Corinth or Rome, instead of churches.

The overseer (bishop) and elders (presbyters) weren't outsiders brought into the local church. Rather, they had generally lived in that community for years. Their strengths and weaknesses were well known to the entire congregation. Furthermore, they didn't qualify to serve as overseers or elders by studying in school and stuffing their heads with knowledge. Rather, the congregation was just as interested in the depth of a leader's *spirituality* as they were in the depth of his knowledge. How close was the man to God? Had he lived for years as an example to other Christians? Was he ready to lay down his life for Christ? As Tertullian told the Romans, "Our presbyters are proven men who obtain their position not by purchase, but by established character."[5]

There were no seminaries. A man learned the necessary skills to be a church leader through the school of experience. He was trained by the existing body of elders, and he learned how to walk closely with God and to shepherd others by seeing and imitating their example. He was given hands-on experience under their supervision and was allowed to make mistakes. He had to be able to teach by example as well as by word before he could even be considered for service as an elder or overseer.

Lactantius explained the difference between Christian and pagan teachers:

> As to anyone who teaches principles to live by and molds the characters of others, I ask, "Is he not obligated himself to live by the principles he teaches?" If he himself does not live by them, his teaching is nullified.... His student will answer him like this, "I cannot practice the things you teach, because they are impossible. You forbid me to be angry. You forbid me to covet. You forbid me to lust. And you forbid me to fear pain and death. This is totally contrary to nature; all living creatures are subject to these emotions. If you are so convinced that it is possible to live contrary to

natural impulses, first let me see you practice the things you teach so I will know they are possible."

...

How will [the teacher] take away this excuse from the self-willed, unless he teaches them by his example, so they can see with their own eyes that the things he teaches are possible. For this very reason, no one obeys the teachings of the philosophers. Men prefer examples to words, because it is easy to speak—but difficult to act.[6]

In one of his letters, Cyprian described the process of selecting a new bishop or overseer: "[He] should be chosen in the presence of the people under the eyes of all, and should be proved worthy and suitable by public judgment and testimony.... For a proper ordination, all the neighboring overseers throughout the same province should assemble with the congregation. The overseer should be chosen in the presence of the congregation, since they are intimately familiar with his life and habits."[7]

Once an elder or overseer was appointed, he normally stayed in that local church for the rest of his life, unless persecution forced him to move. He didn't serve for three or four years and then move to a larger congregation with better compensation. As was mentioned earlier, not only the overseer, but the entire body of elders were normally full-time shepherds and teachers. Unless the congregation was simply too small to support them, elders were expected to free themselves from any secular jobs. By doing so, they could devote their full attention to the flock.

We have copies of a series of letters exchanged between two early congregations concerning the fact that an elder had been named as executor in the will of a deceased Christian. Under Roman law, a person named as executor in someone's will was required to serve, whether he wanted to or not. The task could be extremely time-consuming. The elder was quite shocked that any Christian would name him as executor, since that duty would take him away from his shepherding responsibilities. In fact, the entire body of elders was stunned.[8]

Imagine the benefit to the early Christians of being shepherded by bodies of elders whose sole concern was the spiritual well-being of their congregations. With so many full-time pastors, each member of the congregation undoubtedly received close, individual attention.

To serve as an elder or overseer in the early church, a man had to be willing to lay down everything for Christ. This began with material possessions. An elder didn't leave his secular occupation in exchange for a middle-class salary from the congregation. It was considered heretical for a congregation to pay *any* salary to its overseer or elders. Instead the church financially maintained its leaders on the same basis it supported the widows and orphans. Generally, this meant leaders had the necessities of life and little else.[9]

But leaving behind the material things of the world wasn't their only sacrifice. Elders had to be willing to take the lead in suffering imprisonment, torture, and death. Most of the writers cited in this book were overseers or elders, and more than half of them—Ignatius, Polycarp, Justin Martyr, Hippolytus, Cyprian, Methodius, and Origen—ultimately sacrificed their lives for Christ.

With such extraordinary commitment from their leaders, it's not hard to see why the ordinary Christian of that day was inspired to walk closely with God and to avoid the pattern of the world.

People Of The Cross

No one likes to suffer. I recently read a survey of American people on their views about the national budget deficit. Practically all those interviewed agreed that the deficit had to be reduced. But at the same time, about three-fourths of them were opposed to either raising taxes or cutting federal spending. In other words, they wanted the deficit to go away painlessly. Painless! That's also what we want Christianity to be. Jesus told his disciples, "Anyone who does not take his cross and follow me is not worthy of me. Whoever finds his life, will lose it, and whoever loses his life for my sake will find it" (Matt. 10:38,39). Despite what our Lord told us, the message of the cross is not very popular today. When we share the gospel with nonbelievers, we rarely mention Jesus' words about having to carry our cross. In fact, we often give the impression that once a person accepts Christ, his life will forever be filled with bliss.

In the early church, new believers heard a very different message: being a Christian would entail suffering. These words of Lactantius were typical: "He who chooses to live well for eternity, will live in discomfort for the present. He will be subjected to all types of troubles and burdens as long as he is on earth, so that in the end he will have divine and heavenly consolation. On the other hand, he who chooses to live well for the present will fare badly in eternity."[10] Jesus had similarly contrasted the narrow, cramped road that leads to life with the broad and spacious road leading to destruction. (Matt. 7:13,14)

Ignatius, bishop of Antioch and a companion of the apostle John, was arrested for his Christian testimony. While he was en route to Rome for trial and execution, he wrote letters of admonition and encouragement to several Christian congregations. He told one congregation, "It is necessary, therefore, to not only be called by the name 'Christian' but to actually *be* a Christian.... If we are not ready to die in the same manner of His suffering, His life is not in us"[11] (John 12:25). To another he wrote, "Bring on the fire and the cross. Bring on the packs of wild beasts. Let there be the breaking and dislocating of my bones and the severings of my limbs. Bring on the mutilation of my whole body. In fact, bring on all the diabolical tortures of Satan. Only let me attain to Jesus Christ! ... I would rather die for Jesus Christ than to reign over the ends of the entire earth."[12] Shortly after penning those words, Ignatius was brought before a screaming mob in the Colosseum of Rome, where he was torn to pieces by wild animals.

Tertullian encouraged a group of local Christians who were languishing in a Roman dungeon with these words, "Blessed ones, count whatever is hard in this lot of yours as a discipline of your powers of mind and body. You are about to pass through a noble struggle, in which the living God is your manager and the Holy Spirit is your trainer. The prize is an eternal crown of angelic essence—citizenship in the heavens, glory everlasting." He also told them, "The prison does the same service for the Christian that the desert did for the prophet. Our Lord himself spent much time in seclusion so he would have greater freedom to pray and so he would be away from the world.... *The leg does not feel the chains when the mind is in heaven.*"[13]

But most new believers didn't have to be warned about the coming suffering. They had seen it for themselves. In fact, one of the most powerful means of evangelism in the early church was the example of the thousands of Christians who endured suffering and death because they refused to deny Christ.

In his first apology, Tertullian reminded the Romans that their persecution only strengthened the Christians: "The more you cut us down, the more in number we grow. The blood of Christians is seed.... For after thinking about it, who among you is not eager to find out what is really at the bottom of it all? And after inquiring, who does not end up embracing our teachings? And when he has embraced them, who does not also willingly suffer so that he may partake fully of God's grace?"[14]

"Full gospel." In the twentieth century, this familiar term has come to mean "pentecostal" or "charismatic." However, one of the problems in our churches today is that we rarely hear the *full gospel* preached—regardless of whether or not we are charismatic. We usually hear only the part about blessings; we rarely hear the message of suffering for Christ.

We are so far removed from the message of the early church that most of us have virtually no concept of what it means to suffer *for Christ*. A few years ago I heard a pastor deliver a sermon on the verse, "If you suffer as a Christian, do not be ashamed, but praise God that you bear that name." (1 Pet. 4:16) The pastor commented that most Christians in the United States have no concept of what it means to suffer *as a Christian*.

After the service, I was talking to the pastor when a deacon walked up to him and thanked him for the message. The deacon agreed that most Christians in this country don't understand what it means to suffer for being a Christian. However, the deacon said he knew exactly what it meant. He went on to describe the pain and suffering he had endured a few years previously while undergoing an operation. As I drove home from church, I marveled at how well the deacon had illustrated the very point the pastor was trying to make—we American Christians don't know what it means to suffer for being a Christian. We think when we endure the same tribulations in life common to everyone, we are suffering for Christ.

Of course, there are ways to carry our cross other than enduring persecution. Clement commented that for the average Christian, the cross might be represented by enduring marriage to an unbelieving spouse, obeying unbelieving parents, or suffering as a slave under a pagan master. Although all of those situations could entail much emotional and physical suffering, they were a rather mild form of the cross for anyone who had already committed himself to endure torture and death for Christ (Rom. 8:17; Rev. 12:11).

Although early Christians endured painful marriages to *non-believers*, today thousands of Christians are divorcing their *believing* spouses without hesitation, simply because their marriages are less than ideal. Such persons would rather disobey Christ than to put up with even mild suffering. I've had Christians tell me that they *just couldn't endure* living with their spouse any longer in a marriage marked by constant arguments. I wonder what such people will say on Judgment Day to Christian men and women from the early centuries who were able to endure having a red-hot iron poker gouged into their eyes, or having their arms torn off, or being skinned alive. Why is it that those Christians had the power to endure such excruciating tortures when we often lack the power merely to put up with unpleasant marriages? Maybe it's because we haven't accepted the responsibility of carrying our cross.

Several years ago, a Christian woman who was contemplating divorcing her husband because they were not getting along told me through teary eyes, "I don't want to have to live like this *for the rest of my life.*" Later, I reflected on the expression she had used—*"for the rest of my life."* I thought about the times that I too had used those words. My use of that expression revealed that heaven wasn't a reality to me, at least not in the sense that my life on earth is a reality. The early Christians readily accepted the message of suffering because their eyes were set on eternity. They didn't think in terms of suffering "for the rest of their lives," but as suffering for fifty or sixty years, at the most. The *rest of their lives* would be spent in eternity with Jesus. Compared to that, present trials were inconsequential. Like Tertullian, they realized that "the leg doesn't feel the chains when the mind is in heaven."

Are Humans Capable Of Obeying God?

The early Christians didn't attempt to live such uncompromising lives simply on their own strength. They realized their need for Divine power. Of course, that's nothing new. Throughout the centuries, Christians of all denominations have realized that we need God's help in order to walk by His commandments.

And I don't think any of us have ever deliberately set out to serve God without His help. What frequently happens, however, is something like this: Initially, we do walk closely with God, depending on His power. But we later begin to backslide spiritually and slowly pull away from God. Normally, this process begins internally; outwardly, we still act the same. Although we still go through the motions of one who is depending on God, our prayers begin to become cold and formalized. We may still read the Scriptures, but our minds and hearts are on other interests. In the end, we find ourselves depending entirely on our own strength.

The problem isn't that the church doesn't preach about the need for relying on God's strength. In fact, evangelical Christians generally teach that we are incapable of doing anything good on our own strength. But if we humans are simply unable to obey God, there is nothing we can do about our disobedience—except to pray for God to change us into obedient persons. Yet, does this really work?

I remember my excitement when I first heard someone preach that we can't do anything good by our own power—only God can do good things through us. We only have to ask God to change our faults and to overcome our sins for us. "So this is the secret," I thought to myself. I couldn't wait to put the idea into practice, simply letting God change my faults and eradicate my sins. I prayed eagerly for God to do this very thing. I gave it all to God. Then I waited—but nothing happened. So I prayed more. Still nothing changed.

At first, I thought the problem was just me. Were my prayers not sincere? I finally talked to other Christians in private about the matter and found that I wasn't the only one with this problem. Others had obtained no better results than I had. "So why do you go around saying that God magically takes away our faults and turns us into obedient persons?" I asked them. "Because that's the way it's supposed to work," was the reply. I realized that most Christians were afraid to express themselves honestly about the matter—for fear that they were the only ones who hadn't been successful. So here we were all re-enacting the story of the emperor's new clothes because we were afraid others would consider us unspiritual.

I'm not saying that the sit-back-and-pray approach hasn't ever worked for anyone. I am saying that it hasn't worked for me, and historically it hasn't worked for the church. Our evangelical doctrine on this matter comes from Martin Luther, who taught that we are totally incapable of doing any good by ourselves and that both the desire and power to obey God come from Him alone. Although these were cornerstone teachings of the German Reformation, they didn't produce a German nation of obedient, godly Christians. Rather, just the opposite. Lutheran Germany was a cesspool of drunkenness, immorality, and violence. Sitting back and letting God do *all* the work produced neither a godly church nor a godly nation.[15]

In contrast, the early Christians never taught that humans are incapable of doing good or overcoming sin in their lives. They believed that we *do* have the ability to serve and obey God. However, first we must have a deep love for God and a profound respect for His commandments. As Hermas phrased it, "the Lord has to be in the Christian's heart, not simply on his lips."[16] At the same time, the early Christians didn't believe that they could overcome all of their weaknesses and remain obedient to God day after day simply on their own strength. They needed additional power from God. But it wasn't a matter of sitting back and asking God to do all the work.

They believed that our walk with God is a joint project. The Christian himself must be willing to sacrifice, to pour his energy and very soul into the project. But he also must recognize his need for God's help. As Origen explained, "He makes Himself known to those who, *after doing all that their powers will allow*, confess that they need help from Him."[17]

The early church believed that a Christian must earnestly desire and seek God's help. It wasn't a matter of a one-time request, either, but a continual process. Clement taught his students, "A man by himself working and toiling at freedom from sinful desires achieves nothing. But if he plainly shows himself to be very eager and earnest about this, he attains it by the addition of the power of God. God works together with willing souls. But if the person abandons his eagerness, the spirit from God is also restrained. To save the unwilling is the act of one using compulsion; but to save the willing, that of one showing grace."[18]

So they viewed personal righteousness as a joint project between God and man. There was an infinite supply of power from God; the key was to be able to tap into this power. The earnest desire had to come from the Christian himself. As Origen remarked, we aren't blocks of wood that God manipulates at His fancy.[19] We are human beings capable of desiring God and of responding to Him. In referring to the necessary eagerness on our part, Clement wasn't referring simply to a bare desire. Rather, he said we had to be willing to suffer painful "internal persecution." Putting to death our fleshly ways was going to hurt, and if we weren't willing to suffer internally, wrestling with our sins, then God wasn't going to supply the power (Rom. 8:13; 1 Cor. 9:27).[20]

Some people may be disturbed by this early Christian teaching. But as Jesus said, "Though you do not believe me, believe the works" (John 10:38 NAS). Before we disparage the theology of the early Christians, we had better have a good explanation for their power. We can't deny the fact that they had incredible power. Even the pagan Romans didn't dispute this. As Lactantius declared, "When people see that men are lacerated by various kinds of tortures yet remain unsubdued even when their very torturers are worn out, they come to believe that the agreement of so many and the unyielding faith of the dying is not without meaning. [They realize] that human perseverance alone could not endure such tortures without the aid of God. Even robbers and men of robust frame are unable to endure tortures of this kind.... But among us, boys and delicate women—not to speak of men—silently overcome their torturers. Even the fire is unable to extort a groan from them.... These persons—the young and the weaker sex—do not endure mutilation and burning of their whole bodies because they have no other choice. They could easily avoid this punishment if they wished to [by denying Christ]. But they endure it willingly because they put their trust in God."[21]

There's More To The Story

In summary, the church today could learn some valuable lessons from the early Christians. Three factors enabled them to live as citizens of another kingdom and as people of a different culture: (1) the supportive role of the church, (2) the message of the cross, and (3) the belief that man and God must work together for man's holiness.

I could have ended this book here and let it simply be an inspiring historical sketch. But then I would have told you only half of the story, and the whole story needs to be told. However, I'm going to forewarn you that the rest of the story will probably make you uncomfortable. It did me.

6

What They Believed About Salvation

When I first began studying the early Christian writings, I was surprised by what I read. In fact, after a few days of reading, I put their writings back on the shelf and decided to scrap my research altogether. After analyzing the situation, I realized the problem was that their writings contradicted many of my own theological views.

This is not to say that I found no support for any of my beliefs in the early Christian writings. Their understandings corroborated many of my views. On the other hand, they frequently taught the opposite of what I believed, and they even labeled some of my beliefs as *heretical*. The same would probably hold true of many of your beliefs.

To illustrate, these next few chapters discuss five beliefs that were accepted by nearly all the early Christians. These five examples are not the hardest of their beliefs for us to accept, but neither are they the easiest. You may find that you agree with their views on some of these matters, but it's unlikely that you'll agree on all of them. Please understand that I'm not asking you to accept their teachings on these matters. I'm only asking you to hear them out.

Are We Saved By Faith Alone?

If there's any single doctrine that we would expect to find the faithful associates of the apostles teaching, it's the doctrine of salvation by faith alone. After all, that is *the* cornerstone doctrine of the Reformation. In fact, we frequently say that persons who don't hold to this doctrine aren't really Christians.

The story we usually hear about church history is that the early Christians taught our doctrine of salvation by faith alone. But after Constantine corrupted the church, it gradually began to teach that works play a role in our salvation. Fairly typical of the scenario painted is the following passage from Francis Schaeffer's *How Should We Then Live?* After describing the fall of the Roman Empire and the decline of learning in the West, Schaeffer wrote: "Thanks to the monks, the Bible was preserved—along with sections of Greek and Latin classics.... Nevertheless, the pristine Christianity set forth in the New Testament gradually became distorted. A humanistic element was added: Increasingly, the authority of the church took precedence over the teaching of the Bible. And there was an ever-growing emphasis on salvation as resting on man's meriting the merit of Christ, instead of on Christ's work alone."[1]

Like Schaeffer, most evangelical writers give the impression that the belief that our own merits and works affect our salvation was something that gradually crept into the church *after* the time of Constantine and the fall of Rome. But that's not really the case.

The early Christians universally believed that works or obedience play an essential role in our salvation. This is probably quite a shocking revelation to most evangelicals. But that there's no room for doubt concerning this matter, I have quoted below (in approximate chronological order) from early Christian writers of virtually every generation—from the time of the Apostle John to the inauguration of Constantine:

Clement of Rome, who was a companion of the apostle Paul[2] and overseer of the church in Rome, wrote, "It is necessary, therefore, that we be prompt in the practice of good works. For He forewarns us, 'Behold, the Lord comes and His reward is before His face, to render to every man according to his work.' ... Let us therefore earnestly strive to be found in the number of those who wait for Him, in order that we may share in His promised reward. But how, beloved ones, shall we do this? By fixing our thoughts on God by faith. By earnestly seeking the things that are pleasing and acceptable to Him. By doing the things that are in harmony with His blameless will. And by following the way of truth, casting away from us all unrighteousness and sin."[3]

Polycarp, the personal companion of the apostle John, taught, "He who raised Him up from the dead will also raise us up—if *we do His will and walk in His commandments* and love what He loved, keeping ourselves from all unrighteousness."[4]

The letter of Barnabas states: "He who keeps these [commandments], will be glorified in the kingdom of God; but he who chooses other things will be destroyed with his works."[5]

Hermas, who may have been a contemporary of the apostle John, wrote, "Only those who fear the Lord *and keep His commandments* have life with God. But as to those who do not keep His commandments, there is no life in them.... All, therefore, who despise Him and do not follow His commands deliver themselves to death, and each will be guilty of his own blood. But I implore you to *obey His commands, and you will have a cure for your former sins.*"[6]

In his first apology, written sometime before 150 A.D., Justin Martyr told the Romans, "We have been taught...that He accepts only those who imitate the virtues that reside in Him—self-restraint, justice, and love of mankind.... And so we have received [this teaching] that *if men by their works show themselves worthy of His design,* they are deemed worthy of reigning in company with Him, being delivered from corruption and suffering."[7]

Clement of Alexandria, writing in about 190, said, "The Word, having unveiled the truth, showed to men the summit of salvation, so that either repenting they might be saved, or *refusing to obey*, they might be condemned. This is the proclamation of righteousness: to those who obey, rejoicing; to those who disobey, condemnation."[8] And again, "Whoever obtains [the truth] *and distinguishes himself in good works* shall gain the prize of everlasting life.... Some people correctly and adequately understand how [God provides necessary power], but attaching slight importance to the *works* that lead to salvation, they fail to make the necessary preparation for attaining the objects of their hope."[9]

Origen, who lived in the early 200s, wrote, "The soul... [will] be rewarded according to what it deserves, being destined to obtain either an inheritance of eternal life and blessedness, *if its actions shall have procured this for it*, or to be delivered up to eternal fire and punishments, if the guilt of its crimes shall have brought it down to this."[10]

Hippolytus, a Christian overseer who lived at the same time as Origen, wrote, "The Gentiles, by faith in Christ, prepare for themselves eternal life *through good works*."[11] He again wrote, "[Jesus], in administering the righteous judgment of the Father to all, assigns to each what is righteous *according to his works*.... Justification will be seen in the awarding to each that which is just; to those who have done well, there will be justly assigned eternal happiness. The lovers of wickedness will be assigned eternal punishment.... But the righteous will remember only the *righteous deeds* by which they reached the heavenly kingdom."[12]

Cyprian wrote, "To prophesy, to cast out demons, and to do great acts upon the earth are certainly a sublime and admirable thing. However, a person does not attain the Kingdom of Heaven even though he is found in all these things *unless he walks in the observance of the right and just way.* The Lord says, 'Many will say to me in that day, Lord, Lord, have we not prophesied in your name and cast out demons in your name and performed other powerful works in your name? And then I will confess to them, I never knew you. Depart from me you workers of evil.' [Matt. 7:22,23] There is need of righteousness so one may deserve well of God the Judge. *We must obey His precepts and warnings that our merits may receive their reward.*"[13]

Finally, Lactantius, writing in the early 300s, explained to the Romans, "Why, then, did He make [man] frail and mortal? ... [So] He might set before man virtue, that is, endurance of evils and labors, *by which he might be able to gain the reward of immortality.* For since man consists of two parts, body and soul, of which the one is earthly, the other heavenly, two lives have been assigned to man. The first, which is appointed for the body, is transitory. The other, which belongs to the soul, is everlasting. We received the first at our birth. We attain to the latter by striving, that immortality might not be available to man without some difficulties.... For this reason He has given us this present life, *that we may either lose the true and eternal life by our sins, or win it by our virtue.*"[14]

In fact, *every* early Christian writer who discussed the subject of salvation presented this same view.

Does This Mean That Christians *Earn* Their Salvation By Works?

No, the early Christians did not teach that we earn salvation by an accumulation of good works. They recognized and emphasized the fact that faith is absolutely essential for salvation, and that without God's grace nobody can be saved.

All of the writers quoted above stressed this fact. Here are just a few examples:

Clement of Rome wrote, "[We] are not justified by ourselves. Nor by our own wisdom, understanding, godliness, or works done in holiness of heart. But by that faith through which Almighty God has justified all men since the beginning."[15]

Polycarp wrote, "Many desire to enter into this joy, knowing that 'by grace you are saved, not of works,' but by the will of God through Jesus Christ [Eph. 2:8]."[16]

Barnabas wrote, "To this end the Lord delivered up His flesh to corruption, that we might be sanctified through the remission of sins, which is effected by His blood."[17]

Justin Martyr wrote, "Our suffering and crucified Christ was not cursed by the law. Rather, he made it manifest that He alone would save those who do not depart from His faith.... As the blood of the passover saved those who were in Egypt, so also the blood of Christ will deliver from death those who have believed."[18]

Clement of Alexandria wrote, "It follows that there is one unchangeable gift of salvation given by one God, through one Lord, benefiting in many ways."[19] And again, "Abraham was not justified by works, but by faith [Rom. 4:3]. Therefore, even if they do good works now, it is of no advantage to them after death, if they do not have faith."[20]

Are Faith And Works Mutually Exclusive?

You may be saying to yourself, "I'm confused. Out of one side of their mouths they say we are saved because of our works, and out of the other side they say we are saved by faith or grace. They don't seem to know what they believed!"

Oh, but they did. Our problem is that Augustine, Luther, and other Western theologians have convinced us that there's an irreconcilable conflict between salvation based on grace and salvation conditioned on works or obedience. They have used a fallacious form of argumentation known as the "false dilemma," by asserting that there are only two possibilities regarding salvation: it's either (1) a gift from God or (2) it's something we earn by our works.

The early Christians would have replied that a gift is no less a gift simply because it's conditioned on obedience. Suppose a king asked his son to go to the royal orchard and bring back a basket full of the king's favorite apples. After the son had complied, suppose the king gave his son half of his kingdom. Was the reward a gift, or was it something the son had earned? The answer is that it was a gift. The son obviously didn't earn half of his father's kingdom by performing such a small task. The fact that the gift was conditioned on the son's obedience doesn't change the fact that it was still a gift.

The early Christians believed that salvation is a gift from God but that God gives His gift to whomever He chooses. *And He chooses to give it to those who love and obey him.*

Is their understanding really that strange? I so often hear evangelical Christians say that welfare should only be given to those persons who are truly *deserving*. When they say that certain poor persons are "deserving," do they mean that welfare constitutes wages earned by such persons? Of course not. They still consider welfare to be a gift. Simply because a person is selective in his giving, it doesn't change the gift into a wage.

Yes, But The Bible Says...

Recently when I was explaining the early Christians' understanding of salvation to a group of believers, one of the ladies was a bit disturbed. She exclaimed in annoyance, "It sounds to me like they needed to read their Bibles more!"

But the early Christians *did* read their Bibles. As Josh McDowell points out in *Evidence That Demands a Verdict*:

> J. Harold Greenlee says that the quotations of the Scripture in the works of the early Christian writers "are so extensive that the N. T. [New Testament] could virtually be reconstructed from them without the use of New Testament manuscripts." . . .
>
> Clement of Alexandria (A.D.150-212). 2,400 of his quotes are from all but three books of the New Testament.
>
> Tertullian (A.D.160-220) was a presbyter of the Church in Carthage and quotes the New Testament more than 7,000 times, of which 3,800 are from the Gospels....
>
> Geisler and Nix rightly conclude that "a brief inventory at this point will reveal that there were some 32,000 citations of the New Testament prior to the time of the Council of Nicea (325)."[21]

So please don't accuse the early Christians of not reading their Bibles. These Christians were well aware of what Paul had written concerning salvation and grace. After all, Paul personally taught men like Clement of Rome. However, the early Christians didn't put Paul's letters to the Romans and the Galatians on a pedestal above the teachings of Jesus and the other apostles. They read Paul's words about grace in conjunction with such other Scriptures as:

* "Not everyone who says to me, 'Lord, Lord,' will enter the kingdom of heaven, but only he who does the will of my Father who is in heaven." (Matt. 7:21).

- "He who stands firm to the end will be saved" (Matt.24:13).

- "All who are in their graves will hear his voice and come out—*those who have done good* will rise to live, and those who have done evil will rise to be condemned" (John 5:28,29).

- "Behold, I am coming soon! My reward is with me, and I will give to everyone *according to what he has done*"(Rev. 22:12).

- "Watch your life and doctrine closely. Persevere in them, because if you do, you will save both yourself and your hearers" (1 Tim. 4:16).

Other Scripture passages they cited are listed at the end of this chapter.

So the real issue isn't a matter of *believing* the Scriptures, but one of *interpreting* the Scriptures. The Bible says that "it is by grace you have been saved, through faith—and this not from yourselves, it is the gift of God—not by works" (Eph. 2:8,9). And yet the Bible also says, "You see then how that by works a man is justified and not by faith alone" (Jas. 2:24 KJV). Our doctrine of salvation accepts that first statement but essentially nullifies the second. The early Christian doctrine of salvation gave equal weight to both.

As was pointed out earlier, the early Christians didn't believe that man is totally depraved and incapable of doing any good. They taught that humans are capable of obeying and loving God. But they also believed that for a person to live obediently throughout his entire life, he needed God's power. So obedience wasn't totally dependent on human strength, nor totally dependent on God's power. It was a mixture of both.

To them, salvation was similar. The new birth as spiritual sons of God and heirs of the promise of eternal life is offered to all of us purely as a matter of grace. We do not have to be "good enough" first. We do not have to earn this new birth in any way. And we do not have to atone for all the sins we have committed in our past. The slate is wiped clean through God's grace. We are truly saved by grace, not by works, as Paul said.

Nevertheless, *we* also play a role in our own salvation, according to Scripture and the early Christians. First, we have to *repent* and to *believe* in Christ as our Lord and Savior in order to avail ourselves of God's grace. After receiving the new birth, we also have to *obey* Christ. Yet, obedience itself is still dependent on the continuing grace of God's power and forgiveness. So salvation begins and ends with grace, but in the middle is man's faithful and obedient response. Ultimately, salvation depends on both man and God. For this reason, James could say we are saved by works and not by faith alone.

Can A Saved Person Be Lost?

Since the early Christians believed that our continued faith and obedience are necessary for salvation, it naturally follows that they believed that a "saved" person could still end up being lost. For example, Irenaeus, the pupil of Polycarp, wrote, "Christ will not die again on behalf of those who now commit sin because death shall no more have dominion over Him.... Therefore we should not be puffed up.... But we should beware lest somehow, after [we have come to] the knowledge of Christ, if we do things displeasing to God, we obtain no further forgiveness of sins but rather be shut out from His kingdom"[22] (Heb. 6:4-6).

Tertullian wrote, "Some people act as though God were under an *obligation* to bestow even on the unworthy His intended gift. They turn His liberality into slavery.... For do not many afterwards *fall out of grace? Is not this gift taken away from many*?"[23]

Cyprian told his fellow believers, "It is written, 'He who endures to the end, the same shall be saved' [Matt. 10:22]. So whatever precedes the end is only a step by which we ascend to the summit of salvation. It is not the final point wherein we have already gained the full result of the ascent."[24]

One of the Scripture passages that the early Christians frequently cited is Hebrews 10:26: "If we deliberately keep on sinning after we have received the knowledge of the truth, no sacrifice for sins is left." Our preachers usually tell us that the writer of Hebrews wasn't talking about saved persons. If that's the case, the writer certainly didn't communicate it very effectively to his readers. All the early Christians understood this passage to be talking about persons who had been saved.

Incidentally, some of the quotations from the early Christians might make you think that they lived in eternal *insecurity*. But that's not the case. Although they believed that their heavenly Father could disinherit them if He chose to do so, the overall spirit of their writings show that obedient Christians didn't live with a constant morbid dread of being disinherited. Does an obedient son constantly worry and fret over the possibility of being disinherited by his earthly father?

The Group That Preached Salvation By Grace Alone

As surprising as all of this may be to you, what I'm about to tell you is even more bizarre. There was a religious group, labeled as heretics by the early Christians, who strongly disputed the church's stance on salvation and works. Instead, they taught that man is totally depraved. That we are saved solely by grace. That works play no role in our salvation. And that we cannot lose our salvation once we obtain it.

I know what you're thinking: This group of "heretics" were the real Christians and the "orthodox" Christians were really heretics. But such a conclusion is *impossible*. I say it's impossible because the group I'm referring to are the gnostics.

The Greek word *gnosis* means knowledge, and the gnostics claimed that God had revealed special knowledge to them that the main body of Christians did not have. Although each gnostic teacher had his individual version of teachings, they all basically taught that the Creator was a different God than the Father of Jesus. This inferior God had acted without the authority of the Father in creating the material world. This Creator botched things up and man is inherently depraved as a result. The God of the Old Testament is this inferior Creator who possesses different qualities from the God of the New Testament.

Because humans are the flawed work of this inferior God, they are totally unable to do anything toward their own salvation. Fortunately for mankind, the Father of Jesus took pity on humans and sent his Son for our salvation. However, because the flesh is inherently depraved, the Son could not have actually become a man. Rather, the Son of God simply took on the *appearance* of man. He was not truly man and he never really died or was resurrected. Since everything about man is inherently flawed, our works can play no part in our salvation, but rather we are saved purely by the grace of the Father.[25]

In case you have any lingering doubts on whether the gnostics were true Christians, notice what the Apostle John himself said about them: "Many deceivers, *who do not acknowledge Jesus Christ as coming in the flesh*, have gone out into the world. Any such person is the deceiver and the antichrist" (2 John 7). The gnostics were the ones who denied that Jesus had come in the flesh, and they are the ones to whom John was referring. He made it clear that they were deceivers and antichrists.

So, assuming our evangelical doctrine of salvation to be true, we are faced with the uncomfortable reality that this doctrine was taught by "deceivers and antichrists" before it was taught by the church.

The early Christian understanding of salvation was also based on these passages, among others: "The one who sows to please the Spirit, from the Spirit will reap eternal life. Let us not become weary in doing good, for at the proper time we will reap a harvest if we do not give up" (Gal. 6:9). "For we must all appear in our true characters before the tribunal of the Christ, each to be repaid with good or evil for the life he has lived in the body" (2 Cor 5:10 GSP). "You may be sure that no one who is immoral, or greedy for gain (for that is idolatry) can have any share in the Kingdom of Christ and God" (Eph. 5:5 GSP).

"If we endure, we will reign with him! If we disown him, he will also disown us" (2 Tim. 2:12 GSP). "Let us therefore strive to enter that rest, that no one fall by the same sort of disobedience" (Heb. 4:11 RSV). "You will need endurance if you are to carry out God's will and receive the blessing he has promised" (Heb. 10:36 GSP). "If they have escaped the corruption of the world by knowing our Lord and Savior Jesus Christ and are again entangled in it and overcome, they are worse off at the end than they were at the beginning. It would have been better for them not to have known the way of righteousness, than to have known it and then to turn their backs on the sacred command that was passed on to them" (2 Pet. 2:20,21).

For other Scriptures cited by the early Christians, please see footnote 26.

7

What They Believed About Predestination And Free Will

Many evangelical Christians think that Luther's Reformation returned the church to the standards of the early believers. Many also suppose that today's evangelical Christians are teaching the same things as Luther. However, both of those assumptions are incorrect.

It probably surprised you to learn that our present doctrine of salvation by faith is different from what the early Christians taught. It may surprise you even more to know that our doctrine of salvation is also different from what Martin Luther and other leaders of the Reformation taught. In fact, we teach only *half* of the Reformation doctrine of salvation.

While it's true that Luther sometimes said that man is "saved by faith alone," he also taught that man is so totally depraved that he is unable even to have faith in God or to accept the gift of salvation. Therefore, the only persons who have saving faith are those to whom God has given such faith. And God has given such faith only to those whom he arbitrarily predestined before the creation of the world. By "arbitrarily," I mean that, according to Luther, God's decision to give faith to some, and not to others, wasn't based on any desire, faith, righteousness, actions, or prayers on the part of the recipient.

In the end, Luther could only bemoan, "This is the highest degree of faith—to believe that He is merciful, the very One who saves so few and damns so many. To believe that He is just, the One who according to His own will, makes us necessarily damnable."[1] So the Reformation didn't teach that man is saved by faith alone or that he is saved by accepting Christ. It taught that the predestined are saved by grace alone and the rest of mankind are eternally damned. It's a popular myth that John Calvin introduced this doctrine of predestination, but Calvin was simply repeating established Reformation theology. So today, those who say that the offer of salvation is open to everyone contradict a basic Reformation doctrine.

After the Reformation, evangelical Christians tried for centuries to convince a scoffing world that our lives and eternal fates were arbitrarily predestined by God, and that this was a God we should love. How ironic, therefore, that originally it was the Christians who tried to convince a scoffing world that our lives and fates were *not* predestined.

Believers In Free Will

The early Christians were strong believers in free will. For example, Justin Martyr made this argument to the Romans: "We have learned from the prophets, and we hold it to be true, that punishments, chastisements, and rewards are rendered according to the merit of each man's actions. Otherwise, if all things happen by fate, then nothing is in our own power. For if it be predestined that one man be good and another man evil, then the first is not deserving of praise or the other to be blamed. Unless humans have the power of avoiding evil and choosing good by free choice, they are not accountable for their actions—whatever they may be.... For neither would a man be worthy of reward or praise if he did not of himself choose the good, but was merely created for that end. Likewise, if a man were evil, he would not deserve punishment, since he was not evil of himself, being unable to do anything else than what he was made for."[2]

Clement echoed the same belief: "Neither praise nor condemnation, neither rewards nor punishments, are right if the soul does not have the power of choice and avoidance, if evil is involuntary.[3]

Archelaus, writing a few decades later, repeated the same understanding: "All the creatures that God made, He made very good. And He gave to every individual the sense of free will, by which standard He also instituted the law of judgment.... And certainly whoever will, may keep the commandments. Whoever despises them and turns aside to what is contrary to them, shall yet without doubt have to face this law of judgment.... There can be no doubt that every individual, in using his own proper power of will, may shape his course in whatever direction he pleases."[4]

Methodius, a Christian martyr who lived near the end of the third century, wrote similarly, "Those [pagans] who decide that man does not have free will, but say that he is governed by the unavoidable necessities of fate, are guilty of impiety toward God Himself, making Him out to be the cause and author of human evils."[5]

The early Christians weren't simply speculating about this matter, but rather they based their beliefs on the following Scriptures, among others:

- "For God so loved the world, that he gave his one and only Son, that whoever believes in him shall not perish, but have eternal life" (John 3:16).

- "The Lord is not slow in keeping his promise, as some understand slowness. He is patient with you, *not wanting anyone to perish,* but everyone to come to repentance" (2 Pet. 3:9).

- "The Spirit and the bride say, 'Come!' And let him who hears say, 'Come!' Whoever is thirsty, let him come; and *whoever wishes,* let him take the free gift of the water of life" (Rev. 22:17).

- "I have set before you life and death, blessings and curses. Now *choose* life so that you and your children may live" (Deut. 30:19).

So originally, it was the pagan world, not the Christians, who believed in predestination. Yet, in one of the strange quirks of Christian history, Martin Luther took the side of the pagan Romans against the early Christians. I do not mean that, *in effect,* he took their side. I mean he *literally* sided with them! For example, Luther wrote concerning fate or predestination:

> But why should these things be difficult for we Christians to understand, so that it should be considered irreligious, curious, and vain, to discuss and know them, when heathen poets, and the common people themselves, have them in their mouths in the most frequent use? How often does Virgil [a pagan Roman poet] alone make mention of Fate? "All things stand fixed by unchangeable law." Again, "Fixed is the day of every man." Again, "If the Fates summon you." And again, "If you will break the binding chain of Fate."
>
> The aim of this poet is to show that in the destruction of Troy, and in raising up the Roman empire, Fate did more than all the devoted efforts of men.... From which we can see that the knowledge of predestination and of the foreknowledge of God was no less left in the world than the notion of divinity itself. And those who wished to appear wise went so far into their debates that, their hearts being darkened, they became fools (Rom.

1:21,22). They denied, or pretended not to know those things which their poets, and the common folk, and even their own consciences, held to be universally known, most certain, and most true."[6]

But How Did They Explain Bible Passages That Seem To Teach Predestination?

From what I have observed, many—perhaps most— evangelical Christians say they believe in predestination. Yet, their prayers and actions show they really don't. Others simply throw up their hands, admitting, "I don't know what I believe."

The dilemma we face is that the Bible tells us to 'choose life that we may live,' (Deut. 30:19), but it also tells us that it does not "depend on man's desire or effort, but on God's mercy" (Rom. 9:16). On the one hand, the Scriptures teach that God is patient with us, "not wanting anyone to perish, but *everyone* to come to repentance" (2 Pet. 3:9). But on the other hand, it says, "God has mercy on whom he wants to have mercy, and he hardens whom he wants to harden" (Rom. 9:18).

I have wrestled with these seemingly contradictory passages most of my adult life. So it was very comforting to discover that the early Christians had logical—and Scripturally sound explanations for these seeming contradictions. In fact, their understandings about God's foreknowledge and man's free will are among the most reasonable I've ever heard.

In contrast, it was once again some of the gnostic teachers who taught that humans are arbitrarily predestined for salvation and punishment. Obviously, if we are totally depraved as a result of our being created by an unjust, inferior God (as the gnostics taught), our salvation can only come about by arbitrary election from God. In his work entitled *On First Things*, Origen addressed many of the Scriptural arguments the gnostics were using. He also answered some of the questions about free will and predestination that his students had posed to him. Here is an excerpt from Origen's discussion:

◻ ◻ ◻ ◻ ◻ ◻ ◻ ◻ ◻ ◻

"One of the doctrines included in the teaching of the Church is that there is a just judgment of God. This fact incites those who believe it to live virtuously and to shun sin. They acknowledge that the things worthy of praise and blame are within our own power.

"It is our responsibility to live righteously. God asks this of us, not as though it were dependent on Him, nor on any other, or upon fate (as some think), but as being dependent on us. The prophet Micah demonstrated this when he said, 'It has been announced to you, O man, what is good. And what does the Lord require of you? To do justice and to love mercy' [Mic. 6:8]. Moses also said, 'I have set before you the way of life, and the way of death. Choose what is good and walk in it' [Deut. 30:15].

"Notice how Paul also speaks to us with the understanding that we have freedom of the will and that we ourselves are the cause of our own ruin or our salvation. He says, 'Do you show contempt for the riches of His goodness, patience, and long-suffering, not realizing that God's goodness leads you towards repentance? But because of your stubbornness and your unrepentant heart, you are treasuring up wrath against yourself for the day of wrath and revelation of the righteous judgment of God. God will render to each one according to his works. To those who by persistence in doing good seek glory and immortality, he will give eternal life. But for those who are contentious and who reject the truth and follow evil, there will be anger, wrath and tribulation.' [Rom. 2:4-8].

"But certain statements in the Old and New Testaments might lead to the opposite conclusion: That it does not depend on us to keep the commandments and be saved. Or to transgress them and to be lost. So let's examine them one by one.

"First, the statements concerning Pharaoh have troubled many. God declared several times, 'I will harden Pharaoh's heart' [Exod. 4:21]. Of course, if Pharaoh was hardened by God and sinned as a result of being hardened, he was not the cause of his own sin. So he did not possess free will.

"Along with this passage, let's also look at the passage in Paul: 'But who are you, O man, to talk back to God? Shall the thing formed say to Him who formed it, 'Why have you made me like this?' Does the potter not have power over the clay—from the same lump to make one vessel unto honor, and another unto dishonor?' [Rom. 9:20,21].

"Since we consider God to be both good and just, let's see how the good and just God could harden the heart of Pharaoh. Perhaps by an illustration used by the apostle in the Epistle to the Hebrews, we can show that, by the same operation, God can show mercy to one man while he hardens another, although not intending to harden. 'The ground,' he says, 'drinks in the rain that falls upon it and produces crops for the farmer, being blessed by God. But the ground that produces thorns and briers is worthless, and is in danger of being cursed. Its end is to be burned' [Heb. 6:7,8].

"It may seem strange for Him who produces rain to say, 'I produced both the fruit and the thorns from the earth.' Yet, although strange, it is true. If the rain had not fallen, there would have been neither fruit nor thorns. The blessing of the rain, therefore, fell even on the unproductive land. But since it was neglected and uncultivated, it produced thorns and thistles. In the same way, the wonderful acts of God are like the rain. The differing results are like the cultivated and the neglected land.

"The acts of God are also like the sun, which could say, 'I both soften and harden.' Although these two actions are opposite, the sun would not speak falsely, because the same heat both softens wax and hardens mud. Similarly, on the one hand, the miracles performed through Moses hardened Pharaoh because of his own wickedness. But they softened the mixed Egyptian multitude, who left Egypt with the Hebrews.

"Let's look at another passage: 'So then it is not of him who wills, nor of him that runs, but of God who shows mercy' [Rom. 9:16]. Paul is not denying that something also has to be done by human means. But he gratefully refers the benefit to God, who brings it to completion. The mere human desire is insufficient to attain the end. The mere running does not in itself enable athletes to gain the prize. Nor does it enable Christians to obtain the high calling of God in Christ Jesus. Those things are only accomplished with the assistance of God.

"As if speaking about farming, Paul says, 'I planted, Apollos watered, and God made it grow. So then neither is he who plants anything, nor he that waters, but God, who made it grow' [1 Cor. 3:6,7]. Now we could not correctly say that the growing of crops is the work of the farmer alone. Nor of the one who irrigates. It is ultimately the work of God. Likewise, it is not as though we ourselves play no role in our spiritual growth to perfection. Yet, it is not completed by us, for God produces the greater part of it. So also with our salvation. What God does is infinitely greater than what we do."[7]

◻ ◻ ◻ ◻ ◻ ◻ ◻ ◻ ◻ ◻

Can God Foresee The Future?

Although not believing in predestination, the early Christians strongly believed in God's sovereignty and in His ability to foresee the future. For example, they understood God's prophecies about Jacob and Esau to be a result of His foreseeing the future, not a result of His arbitrarily predestining those men to a particular fate. But they saw a significant distinction between *foreseeing* something and *causing* it.

8

What Baptism Meant To The Early Christians

I still remember the first time I read Jesus' words to Nicodemus: "Truly I say to you, unless one is born of water and the Spirit, he cannot enter the kingdom of God" (John 3:5 NAS). I was a young boy at the time, and I was reading that verse in a small Bible study group. The teacher asked the question, "What does it mean to be born of 'water'?" I thought for a moment and quickly raised my hand. "Jesus must have been referring to water baptism," I blurted out, feeling proud of myself for having figured this out. However, to my chagrin, the teacher explained that this was a common misconception and that 'being born of water' was not water baptism.

Through the years I was able to correct others who mistakenly thought that this passage refers to water baptism. I felt very knowledgeable to be able to explain the "correct" view. So it took the wind out of my sails when I discovered that the early Christians *universally* understood Jesus' words to refer to water baptism.

And once again, it was the gnostics who taught differently than the church—saying that humans can't be reborn or regenerated through water baptism. Irenaeus wrote about them: "This class of men have been instigated by Satan to a denial of that baptism which is regeneration to God."[1]

In today's evangelical church, water baptism is often regarded as a rather insignificant matter, at least in the process of salvation. However, baptism carried the utmost significance to the early Christians. They associated three very important matters with water baptism:

1. Remission of sins. They believed that water baptism canceled all past sins. For example, Justin Martyr wrote, "There is no other way [to obtain God's promises] than this—to become acquainted with Christ, to be washed in the fountain spoken of by Isaiah for the remission of sins, and for the remainder, to live sinless lives."[2]

They based their views on baptism and remission of sin on the following Bible passages, among others:

- "And now what are you waiting for? Get up, be baptized and *wash your sins away*, calling on his name" (Acts 22:16).

- "He saved us, not because of righteous things we had done, but because of His mercy. *He saved us through the washing of rebirth* and renewal by the Holy Spirit" (Titus 3:5).

- "Corresponding to that, *baptism now saves you*—not the removal of dirt from the flesh, but an appeal to God for a good conscience" (1 Pet. 3:21 NAS).

- "Repent, and let each of you be baptized in the name of Jesus Christ *for the forgiveness of your sins*" (Acts 2:38 NAS).

Since this washing was completely independent of any merit on the baptized person's part, baptism was frequently referred to as "grace." I was surprised to find that the early Christians used the term "grace" to refer to a specific act such as baptism. Several years ago when our adult Sunday School class was studying the beliefs of the Roman Catholic Church, we discussed their use of the word "grace" to refer to sacraments administered by the priest. I remember thinking to myself, "Catholics sure can get things fouled up!" I realize now that the Catholic use of the term may be more akin to the way the New Testament Christians understood the word.

2. The New Birth. Based on Jesus' words to Nicodemus, the early Christians also believed water baptism was the channel through which a person was born again. Irenaeus mentioned this in a discussion about baptism, "As we are lepers in sin, we are made clean from our old transgressions by means of the sacred water and the invocation of the Lord. We are thus spiritually regenerated as newborn infants, even as the Lord has declared: 'Except a man be born again through water and the Spirit, he shall not enter into the kingdom of heaven'"[3] [John 3:5].

3. Spiritual Illumination. The early Christians believed that the newly-baptized person, after receiving the Holy Spirit, had a clearer vision of spiritual matters, receiving illumination as a child of God and a citizen of His kingdom.

Clement of Alexandria discussed all three of these spiritual events associated with baptism: "This work is variously called grace, and illumination, and perfection, and washing. Washing, by which we cleanse away our sins. Grace, by which the penalties of our sins are canceled. And illumination, by which that holy light of salvation is beheld, that is, by which we see God clearly."[4]

In a letter to a young Christian friend, Cyprian explained his own baptism in a similar fashion, "Considering my character at the time, I used to regard it as a difficult matter that a man should be able to be born again.... Or that a man who had been revived to a new life in the bath of saving water could be able to put off what he had formerly been—that he could be changed in heart and soul, while retaining his physical body.... I used to indulge my sins as if they were actually a part of me, inherent in me. But later, by the help of the water of new birth, the stain of former years was washed away, and a light from above—serene and pure was infused into my reconciled heart. Then through the Spirit breathed from heaven, a second birth restored me to a new man."[5]

Baptism Was Not An Empty Ritual

In short, baptism in early Christianity was the supernatural rite of initiation by which a new believer passed from being the old man of the flesh to being a newly reborn man of the spirit. However, please don't think their practice was some empty ritual. The early Christians didn't separate baptism from faith and repentance. Baptism wasn't some magical ritual that could regenerate a person if it wasn't accompanied by faith and repentance. They specifically taught that God was under no necessity to grant forgiveness of sins simply because a person went through the motions of baptism.[6] A faithless person was not reborn through water baptism.

In his *First Apology*, Justin Martyr explained to the pagans how faith, repentance, and baptism were inseparably intertwined: "Those who are convinced that what we teach is true and who desire to live accordingly are instructed to fast and to pray to God for the remission of all their past sins. We also pray and fast with them. Then we bring them to a place where there is water, and they are regenerated in the same manner in which we ourselves were regenerated. They then receive the washing with water in the name of God (the Father and Lord of the universe) and of our Savior Jesus Christ, and of the Holy Spirit. For Christ said, 'Unless you are born again, you shall not enter into the kingdom of heaven'"[7] [John 3:5].

Were Unbaptized Persons Automatically Damned?

One thing that particularly impresses me about the early Christians is that they never put God in a box. For example, they always believed that God would do what was loving and just toward pagans who had never had the opportunity to hear about Christ. Likewise, they believed that although baptism was the normal channel of grace and the means of rebirth, God was not necessarily bound by it. For instance, they believed that unbaptized babies who died in infancy could still be saved. It was Augustine, writing centuries later, who taught that all unbaptized infants are damned.

Another example was that of martyrs. Many new believers were martyred before they ever had a chance to be baptized. The early church knew that the God of love would not abandon such persons. The church said that, in a sense, they had been baptized in a baptism of blood. So although early Christians stressed the significance of baptism and its role in the new birth, they didn't portray God as a cold, inflexible Being who could work no other way.

The Evangelical Rite Of Passage

Interestingly, we evangelicals seem to recognize the need for some type of initiation ceremony or rite of passage to mark the Christian rebirth. But strangely enough, we have generally rejected the historical ceremony of the baptismal rebirth and have developed our own special ceremony—the altar call. When Peter preached to the Jews on the day of Pentecost, his hearers asked him, "What shall we do?" (Acts 2:37). Did Peter tell them to walk up to the front of the crowd and invite Jesus to come into their hearts? No, he told them, "Repent, and let each of you be *baptized* in the name of Jesus Christ for the forgive-ness of your sins" (Acts 2:38 NAS).

After Philip explained the gospel to the Ethiopian eunuch, what did he do? He immediately baptized him (Acts 8:34-38). Likewise, when God demonstrated to Peter (by the outpouring of the Spirit on Cornelius) that Christianity was open to Gentiles, the first thing that Peter did was to baptize Cornelius and his family (Acts 10:44-48). When Paul preached in the middle of the night to the Philippian jailer and his household, did Paul then hold an altar call? No! The Scriptures say, "Then they spoke the word of the Lord to him and to all the others in his house. At that hour of the night the jailer took them and washed their wounds; then *immediately* he and all his family were baptized" (Acts 16:32,33).

Since we feel the need to associate our spiritual rebirth with a fixed day and hour, why don't we tie it to baptism, rather than to the altar call? Actually, the altar call and associate prayers are a product of the revival movements of the eight-eenth and nineteenth centuries, and they were unknown to any Christians before that time.

9

Prosperity: A Blessing Or A Snare

The pastor of the largest church in the world, Dr. Paul Yonggi Cho, recently wrote a book on the subject of Christian prosperity. He entitled it *Salvation, Health and Prosperity.* After discussing the fact that we are citizens of heaven, he went on to declare, "If we are kings, shouldn't we have majesty, honor and material things befitting kings? This is our natural inheritance. It is a legacy which we can claim by showing the proper credentials. These are our treasures which we can claim as easily as we would draw money from a bank in which a generous amount of money had been deposited in our name with our account number on it. If one professes to be a king, but is impoverished and helplessly sick in bed, how can people believe he is a king?"[1]

The "health and wealth gospel" is extremely popular in the church today. Many of the fastest growing churches in America and throughout the world preach this "gospel." Some prosperity preachers build an entire theology around one verse from the Third Letter of John: "Beloved, I pray that in all respects you may prosper and be in good health, just as your soul prospers" (3 John 2 NAS).

What did John mean by those words? Was he saying that he wanted his fellow Christians to be materially prosperous and physically healthy? Was he promising them riches and health from God?

Before conjecturing about the meaning of John's words, why doesn't anyone bother to consult the writings of Polycarp, John's close companion? If our prosperity preachers had checked the writings of John's companion, they would have found an urgent warning against seeking material prosperity—not a message of physical health and material wealth. In fact, the early Christians testify that the apostles themselves lived in poverty, not material wealth.

Rather than viewing wealth as a promised blessing from God, the early Christians viewed it as an entanglement that could cost a Christian his eternal life. They based this understanding on Scripture passages such as:

- "The love of money is a root of all kinds of evil" (1 Tim. 6:10).

- "Keep your lives free from the love of money and be content with what you have" (Heb. 13:5).

- "Do not store up for yourselves treasures on earth... but store up for yourselves treasures in heaven... for where your treasure is, there your heart will be also" (Matt. 6:19-21).

- "No one can serve two masters. Either he will hate the one and love the other, or he will be devoted to the one and despise the other. You cannot serve both God and Money" (Matt. 6:24).

Some of the other Scriptures they relied on are set forth at the end of this chapter.

The Dangers Of Prosperity

Applying some of the verses cited above, Hermas wrote, "These are those who have faith indeed, but also have the riches of this world. When tribulation comes, they deny the Lord on account of their riches and business.... As a result, those who are rich in this world cannot be useful to the Lord unless their riches are first cut down. Learn this first from your own case. When you were rich, you were useless. But now you are useful and fit for life."[2] He therefore advised, "Refrain from much business and you will avoid sin. Those who are occupied with much business also commit many sins, being distracted by their business affairs instead of serving their Lord."[3]

Clement warned that "wealth can single-handedly puff up and corrupt the souls of those who possess it and turn them from the path of salvation." He described wealth as "a weight that ought to be removed and taken away as though it were a dangerous and deadly disease."[4]

Cyprian, a wealthy man who gave all his goods to the poor upon becoming a Christian, admonished the members of his congregation with these words: "A blind love of one's own property has deceived many. How could they be prepared for, or comfortable with, departing this earth [in persecution] when their wealth fettered them like a chain?... Therefore, the Lord, the teacher of good things, forewarning for the future, says, 'If you will be perfect, go, sell all you have, and give to the poor, and you shall have treasure in heaven. And come and follow me' [Matt. 19:21]. If rich men did this, they would not perish by their riches.... Heart, mind and feeling would be in heaven, if the treasure were in heaven. [Matt. 6:21] He who had nothing in the world would not be overcome by the world. He would follow the Lord unfettered and free, as the apostles did.... But how can they follow Christ when they are held back by the chain of their wealth?... *They think that they own, when actually it is they who are owned.* They are not the lords of their money, but rather the slaves of money."[5]

Drawing from Jesus' illustration of the broad and the narrow roads, Lactantius warned against those who promised wealth and prosperity:

◻ ◻ ◻ ◻ ◻ ◻ ◻ ◻ ◻ ◻

Satan, having invented false religions, turns men away from the heavenly path and leads them into the way of ruin. That path seems to be level and spacious and delightful with all kinds of flowers and fruits. For Satan places on this path all the things which are esteemed on earth as good things—wealth, honor, leisure, pleasure, and all sorts of enticements. But hidden along with these are also injustice, cruelty, pride, lust, fights, ignorance, falsehood, folly, and other vices. But the end of this way is as follows: When they have reached the point of no return, it is suddenly removed, along with its beauty. It is so sudden that no one is able to foresee this fraud before he falls headfirst into a deep abyss....

In contrast, the heavenly path seems to be difficult and hilly, covered with painful thorns and strewn with jagged rocks. As a result, everyone must walk with the greatest care and must take precautions against falling. On this road, God has placed justice, self-restraint, patience, faith, chastity, self-control, peace, knowledge, truth, wisdom, and other virtues. But along with these go poverty, lowliness, work, pain, and all kinds of hardships. For whoever has extended his hope beyond the present life and chosen better things, will be without these earthly goods. Because he is lightly equipped and free of hindrances, he can overcome the difficulty of the way. For it is impossible for the man who has surrounded himself with royal pomp, or loaded himself with riches, either to enter this path or to persevere in the face of these difficulties [Matt. 7:13,14;19:23,24]."[6]

◻ ◻ ◻ ◻ ◻ ◻ ◻ ◻ ◻ ◻

But the early Christians didn't just *talk* about poverty, the majority of them *were* poor. And the Romans ridiculed them for it. For example, one Roman taunted the Christians, "See many of you—in fact, by your own admission, the majority of you—are in want, are cold, are hungry, and are laboring in hard work. Yet, your God allows it."[7] Admitting the truthfulness of this accusation, the Christian lawyer Mark Felix answered: "That many of us are called poor, this is not our disgrace, but our glory. As our mind is relaxed by luxury, it is strengthened by poverty. Yet who can be poor if he does not long for anything? If he does not crave the possessions of others? If he is rich towards God? He rather is poor, who, although he has much, desires more."[8]

The anti-materialistic message of Christianity was so strange to the Romans that they ridiculed Christianity. The Roman critic Celsus asked the Christians, "How could God command [the Jews] through Moses to gather wealth, to extend their dominion, to fill the earth, [and] to put their enemies of every age to the sword.... while on the other hand, His Son, the man of Nazareth, gave laws quite opposite to these. He declared that no one can come to the Father if he loves power, riches, or glory. That men should no more worry about obtaining food than the ravens. That they should be less concerned about their clothing than the lilies."[9]

Someone might argue that these Christians lived in poverty only because they rejected God's prosperity and gave their wealth away. But how can a person out give God? If wealth is from God, a Christian can't lose it by obeying God's Word and sharing his wealth with the poor.

What A Contrast Between Their Message And Today's Message!

Now contrast the teachings of the early Christians with what is being taught in so many churches today. For example,

Kenneth Hagin, a popular Christian preacher and writer in America today, claims to have had this conversation with God:

□ □ □ □ □ □ □ □ □ □

"The Lord continued, 'You say, "Satan, take your hands off my money!" because it's Satan who is keeping it from coming to you—not Me.

"'Claim it because it's down there on earth and Satan has the most control of it, because he's the god of this world. Say, "I claim....," naming whatever it is you want or need.'

"People will argue, 'Well, I can believe that God will meet our *needs*, but that's getting too far out when you start talking about *wants!*' That's just what I said to the Lord. 'Now, Lord, I can believe that You want to meet our needs—but our wants?'

"He replied, 'You claim to be a stickler for the Word. In the 23rd Psalm that you quote so many times, it says, "The Lord is my shepherd; I shall not WANT.'

"It says in the 34th Psalm, 'The young lions do lack, and suffer hunger: but they that seek the Lord shall not WANT any good thing.' (v.10).

Claim whatever you need or want. Say, 'Satan, take your hands off my finances.' Then say, 'Go, ministering spirits, and cause the money to come.'"[10]

□ □ □ □ □ □ □ □ □ □

However, in the first few centuries, it was the *heretics,* not the church, who taught prosperity theology. For example, one of the most infamous heretics of the third century, Paul of Samosata, both taught and practiced a message of wealth. A group of elders living in his day described him this way: "Formerly, he was destitute and poor. He inherited no wealth from his father. He did not acquire anything by trade or business. But now he possesses abundant wealth through his wrongdoing and sacrilegious acts.... He has made [his followers] rich. Because of this he is loved and admired by those who desire such things."[11]

Did Christians Enjoy Better Health?

As to the "gospel of health," the records of both secular and Christian history show that early Christians enjoyed no better health than the world around them. Letters written by early Christians testify to the fact that Christians suffered from the same plagues and calamities as the rest of mankind.

Early Christians believed in divine healing, but their testimonies about healing miracles indicate that such miracles were primarily administered to non-believers as a sign. They weren't something Christians normally received as a promised blessing.

Cyprian discussed the fact that some Christians were disappointed when they suffered from a severe plague:

> It disturbs some that the power of this disease attacks our people in the same way it attacks the pagans. As if the Christian believed in order to have the pleasures of the world and a life free from illness, instead of enduring adversity here and awaiting a future joy. As long as we are here on the earth, we experience the same fleshly tribulations as the rest of the human race, although we are separated in spirit.... So when the earth is barren with an unproductive harvest, famine makes no distinction. When an invading army captures a city, all are taken as captives alike. When the serene clouds withhold rain, the drought is alike to all.... We have eye diseases, fevers, and feebleness of the limbs the same as others.[12]

Early Christianity wasn't a religion that promised material prosperity and better health in *this* life. Yet the early Christians surely believed in the power of God. As earlier chapters have shown, their faith in the power and protection of God surpassed the trust of most Christians today.

However, their clash with us went far beyond the issue of prosperity. They clashed with us on several moral issues that face the church today.

Other Scriptures concerning material wealth are: "You still lack one thing. Sell everything you have and give to the poor, and you will have treasure in heaven. Then come, follow Me" (Luke 18:22). "Indeed, it is easier for a camel to go through the eye of a needle than for a rich man to enter the kingdom of God" (Luke 18:25). "For everything in the world—the cravings of sinful man, the lust of his eyes and the boasting of what he has and does—comes not from the Father but from the world" (1 John 2:16). "If we have food and clothing, with these we shall be content" (1 Tim. 6:8 RSV). "Come now, you rich people! Weep aloud and howl over the miseries that are going to overtake you! Your wealth has rotted.... and their rust will testify against you and eat into your very flesh, for you have stored up fire for the last days" (Jas. 5:1-3 GSP). "Now the overseer must be above reproach, ... not a lover of money" (1 Tim. 3:2,3). "Command those who are rich in this present world not to be arrogant nor to put their hope in wealth, which is so uncertain" (1 Tim. 6:17).

10

Do The Moral Teachings Of The New Testament Surpass Those Of The Old?

Are the moral principles of the New Testament actually different from those of the Old? John Calvin, the sixteenth century church reformer and theologian, taught very emphatically that they were *not*. In one of his treatises against the Anabaptists, he wrote, "The only subterfuge left to these enemies of all order is to claim that our Lord requires a greater perfection in the Christian church than He did of the Jewish people. Now that is true with respect to the ceremonies. But that there exists a different rule of life with respect to the moral law—as it is called—than the people of old had is a false opinion.... Therefore, let us hold this position.... with regard to a faithful man walking in good conscience and being whole before God in both his vocation and in all his works, there exists a plain and complete guideline for it in the law of Moses, to which we need simply cling if we want to follow the right path. Thus whoever adds to or takes anything from it exceeds the limits. Therefore, our position is sure and infallible."[1]

Although most of us would perhaps not be as dogmatic as Calvin, evangelicals today generally hold to his view that, with the exception of dietary and ceremonial distinctions, there is little or no difference between the moral precepts of the Old Testament and the New Testament. In fact, we frequently cite the Old Testament in support of our views on principles for Christian living.

However, the understanding of the early Christians was that the moral teachings of Christ *surpassed* the moral teachings of the Old Testament. The church didn't believe that God Himself had changed, only that the teachings of Christ went to the core of the Law and tapped its true spiritual meaning. Furthermore, they believed that the commandments of the Old Testament were for an earthly kingdom, but the teachings of the New Testament are for citizens of a heavenly kingdom. As a result, they applied Jesus' moral teachings quite literally—which led to some attitudes and practices that are quite different from ours

Previous chapters have shown how they carefully followed New Testament teachings on such topics as divorce, wealth, and lawsuits. Here are some additional examples:

What Did Jesus Mean When He Said "Do Not Swear"?

In the Sermon on the Mount, Jesus taught: "You have heard that it was said to the people long ago, 'Do not break your oath, but keep the oaths you have made to the Lord.' But I tell you, Do not swear at all" (Matt. 5:33,34). James wrote similarly: "Above all, my brothers, do not swear—not by heaven or by earth or by anything else. Let your "Yes" be yes, and your "No," no, or you will be condemned" (Jas. 5:12). Before reading the early Christian writings, I was aware that a few Christian denominations took Jesus' words literally and refused to take oaths. I had always viewed such denominations as taking Jesus' words too literally, and I expected to find support for my interpretation in the early Christian writings.

But, instead, I found that early Christians uniformly refused to take oaths. As Clement remarked, "How can he who is faithful show himself to be unfaithful, so as to require an oath? ... But he does not even swear, preferring to affirm by saying 'yes' or deny by [saying] 'no.'"[2] Tertullian explained to the Romans, "I need say nothing about false swearing, since even swearing is not lawful."[3] Origen, Cyprian, and Eusebius also verify that this was the standard position of the early Christians as to swearing.[4]

Is War Morally Wrong?

Before I began studying the early Christian writings, I had read in church history books that the early Christians generally refused military service. Those books said the early Christians weren't opposed to bloodshed; rather, they rejected military service in order to avoid participating in idolatrous practices. But that's not true. In their writings, the early Christians clearly stated they opposed war because they literally followed Jesus' commandments to "love your enemies" and "turn the other cheek." They viewed war as *morally wrong.*

Justin Martyr wrote in his apology to the Romans, "We who formerly murdered one another now refrain from making war upon our enemies."[5]

Tertullian raised the following question about war: "Can it be lawful to make an occupation of the sword, when the Lord proclaims that 'he who uses the sword shall perish by the sword'? And shall the son of peace take part in battle, when it does not become him even to sue at law? Shall he apply the chain, the prison, the torture, and the punishment, when he is not the avenger of his own wrongs?"[6] (Matt. 26:52; 1 Cor. 6:1-8).

When pagans began circulating a rumor that Christianity was a sect that had broken away from Judaism by armed revolt, Origen answered this false charge with these words, "Nowhere does He teach that it is right for His own disciples to offer violence to anyone, however wicked. For He deemed the killing of *any* individual to be against His laws, which were divine in origin. If Christians had owed their origins to a rebellion, they would not have adopted laws of so exceedingly mild a character. [These laws] do not even allow them on any occasion to resist their persecutors, even when they are called to be slaughtered as sheep."[7]

Cyprian made the following observation about war: "The whole world is wet with mutual blood. Murder, which is admitted to be a *crime* when it is committed by an individual, is called a *virtue* when it is committed wholesale. Impunity is claimed for the wicked deeds [of war], not because they are guiltless, but because the cruelty is perpetrated on a grand scale."[8]

Arnobius, an apologist living in the third century, explained the Christian position to the Romans in this manner, "We have learned from His teaching and His laws that evil should not be repaid with evil [Rom. 12:17]. That it is better to suffer wrong than to inflict it. And that our own blood should be shed rather than to stain our hands and our conscience with that of another. As a result, an ungrateful world has now for a long period been enjoying a benefit from Christ. For by His means the rage of savage ferocity has been softened, and the world has begun to withhold hostile hands from the blood of a fellow creature."[9]

At a time when military valor was considered to be the greatest of virtues, the early Christians stood alone in declaring that war was simply murder on a grand scale. How ironic, therefore, that evangelical Christians in the United States not only condone war but are generally more militaristic than other segments of society. We are often labeled as "war mongers" by the world. In fact, I know of no war in the entire history of the

United States that evangelical Christians opposed in any significant numbers.

When the Iranian crisis of 1980 erupted, I was a law student at Baylor University, a Southern Baptist college. The day after Americans at the U.S. embassy in Tehran were taken hostage, I saw several students from the Middle East in the school cafeteria. I didn't know the nationality of the students; more than likely, they weren't even Iranians. Nevertheless, as various American students walked past their table, the Americans purposefully bumped into their table as a threatening gesture. In the cafeteria and corridors, I overheard vehement discussions of how the United States ought to send our armies to Iran and "stomp those sand niggers in the ground." How sad that when the chips were down, Christians reacted with the same anger and hate as the world.

But Doesn't A Christian Have A Responsibility To His Country?

"Shouldn't a Christian help to defend his country?" you may ask. The early Christians would have answered, "Yes—but in a very different way than the world." The Romans made the same charge to the early Christians, and the Christians replied:

◻◻◻◻◻◻◻◻◻◻

"We are urged 'to help the king with all our might, to work with him in the preservation of justice, to fight for him, and if he requires it to fight under him, or to lead an army along with him.'

"Our answer is that we do, when occasion requires, give help to kings, but in a divine way, 'putting on the whole armor of God.' We do this in obedience to the injunction of the apostle, 'I urge, therefore, first of all, that supplications, prayers, intercessions and thanksgiving be made for all men—for kings and for all those in authority' [1 Tim. 2:1,2].

The more anyone excels in holiness, the more effective is his help to kings, even more than is given by soldiers who go out to fight and slay as many of the enemy as they can.

"To those enemies of our faith who would require us to bear arms for the empire and to slay men, we reply, "Do not the priests who attend [your gods] ... keep their hands free from blood, so that they may offer the appointed sacrifices to your gods with hands unstained and free from human blood?' Even when war is upon you, you never enlist the priests in the army. If, then, that is a praiseworthy custom, how much more so that while others are engaged in battle, [Christians] too should engage as the priests and ministers of God, keeping their hands pure.... By our prayers we vanquish all demons who stir up war.... In this way, we are much more helpful to the kings than those who go into the field to fight for them.... And none fight better for the king than we do. *Indeed, we refuse to fight under him, even if he demands it.* But we do fight on his behalf, forming a special army—an army of righteousness—by offering our prayers to God."[10]

◼ ◻ ◼ ◻ ◼ ◻ ◼ ◻ ◼ ◻

We may be inclined to call their view unrealistic; the early Christians called it *trust*. Who is right? History would indicate that perhaps these Christians weren't as naive as they might seem to us. During the period from the birth of Christ to close to the beginning of the third century, the Roman Empire didn't experience even one successful invasion of its frontiers. Historians call this the Pax Romana (Roman Peace) and view it as a rather extraordinary period in the history of Western civilization. For 200 years, the ancient Mediterranean world enjoyed peace—something it did not have before the Pax Romana and something it has never had since. Of course, no secular historian would credit this peace to the presence and prayers of the Christians, but the early Christians firmly believed that it was a result of Divine intervention.

For example, Origen asked the Romans, "How, then, was it possible for the Gospel doctrine of peace, which does not permit men to take vengeance even upon their enemies, to prevail throughout the world, unless at the coming of Jesus a milder spirit had been introduced everywhere into the conduct of things?"[11]

In contrast, after the time of Constantine, when Christian teachers such as Augustine began teaching the doctrine of "holy war" and Christians supported Rome with the sword, the entire western Roman Empire collapsed within a few decades. Did the Roman Empire fall because the church changed its position on war? No human can answer that question with certainty. But at the very least, it's certainly a remarkable coincidence that Rome prospered and was safe from its enemies so long as the Christians served as a "special army of righteousness," trusting only in God for the empire's protection—and that once Christians began to wage physical war on behalf of Rome, the empire collapsed.

Can A Christian Be In The Military?

Consistent with its position of not legislating righteousness in other areas of life, the early church made no law that Christians could not serve in the army. The Scriptures only commanded a Christian to love his enemies and not to return evil for evil. Neither Jesus nor the apostles ever strictly forbade Christians to serve in the military. Since the Roman Empire was at peace during this early period of Christianity, it was quite possible for a Christian to spend his entire life in the army and never be required to shed blood. In fact, during this period, soldiers primarily served in a capacity similar to American police officers. Generally speaking, the church did not permit a Christian to join the army *after* his conversion. However, if a man was already a soldier when he became a Christian, the church did not require him to resign. He was only required to agree to never use the sword against anyone. One reason for this flexibility was that the Romans did not normally allow a soldier to leave the army until his time of service was completed.[12]

How Should A Christian View Capital Punishment?

God ordained capital punishment in the laws He gave to the Israelites. For that reason, I've always been a strong supporter of capital punishment, and I expected to find that the early Christians were, too. So I was rather surprised to find that the early Christians viewed capital punishment much the same way they viewed war.

Although only a few writers discussed the subject, every one of them expressed the same view: a Christian should not execute a criminal, watch public executions in the arena (something the Romans delighted in), or even bring a capital charge against a fellow human being. In short, the early Christians utterly abhorred the taking of human life whether by war, execution, or abortion.

For instance, Lactantius wrote, "When God forbids us to kill, he not only prohibits the violence that is condemned by public laws, but he also forbids the violence that is deemed lawful by men. Thus it is not lawful for a just man to engage in warfare, since his warfare is justice itself. Nor is it [lawful] to accuse anyone of a capital offense. It makes no difference whether you put a man to death by word, or by the sword. It is the act of putting to death itself which is prohibited. Therefore, regarding this precept of God there should be no exception at all. Rather, it is always unlawful to put to death a man, whom God willed to be a sacred creature."[13]

However, Christians did not purport to tell the secular government what it could or could not do in punishing criminals. The early Christians recognized that God allowed secular governments to use the sword, as His "avenger who brings wrath upon the one who practices evil" (Rom. 13:4 NAS). However, the early Christians believed that they could not in any way personally participate in the execution of criminals.

So Who Are The Real Heretics?

Once again, the early Christians showed themselves to be citizens of a heavenly kingdom and a people of a different culture. And once more we find today's evangelical Christianity far removed from early Christianity. As I mentioned previously, the teachings discussed in this chapter and the four preceding ones, are merely examples of early Christian beliefs that differ radically from our evangelical teachings. There are many, many more examples that could be given. We label as heresy many of the doctrines they taught. They labeled as heresy many doctrines we teach. Who are the real heretics?

Other passages they cited on war were: "All who draw the sword will die by the sword'" (Matt. 26:52). "My kingdom is not of this world. If it were, my servants would fight to prevent my arrest by the Jews. But now my kingdom is from another place" (John 18:36). "For though we live in the world, we do not wage war as the world does. The weapons we fight with are not the weapons of the world" (2 Cor. 10:3,4). "Our struggle is not against flesh and blood, but against the rulers, against the authorities.... Therefore, put on the full armor of God" (Eph. 6:12,13). "Bless your persecutors; bless them; do not curse them.... Do not pay anyone back with evil for evil.... If possible, for your part, live peaceably with everybody. Do not take your revenge, dear friends, but leave room for God's anger.... Do not be conquered by evil, but conquer evil with good" (Rom. 12:17-21 GSP). "When people abuse us, we bless them." (1 Cor. 4:12 GSP).

11

Who Better Understands The Apostles?

We evangelical Christians today generally think that we are following apostolic Christianity. The early Christians thought they were too. Yet, as we've seen, our beliefs and practices vary considerably from theirs. So how can we know which one of us is more closely following the pattern set by the apostles?

A tempting, but simplistic solution is to say, "Let's simply compare their beliefs and ours to what the Bible teaches." The problem is that the early Christians based their beliefs on the Bible—the same as we do. They quoted Scriptures to support their beliefs, the same as we do. The real issue is one of Bible *interpretation*. The most we can do is to compare their interpretations of Scripture with our interpretations of Scripture. And that in itself doesn't prove very much.

So the question becomes: Whose interpretation is more likely to be correct—ours or theirs?

The Advantage Of Time

Interestingly, the early church faced a stand-off with the gnostics that was similar to our stalemate with the early Christians. Both the church and the gnostics claimed they had the true gospel. Tertullian wrote, "I say that *my* gospel is the true one. Marcion [a leading gnostic teacher] says that *his* is. I say that Marcion's gospel is adulterated. He says mine is. Now, how can we settle this stand-off, unless we use the principle of *time.* According to this principle, authority lies with the one who is prior in time. It's based on the elemental truth that corruption (of doctrine) lies with the one who is shown to have originated later in time. Since error is falsification of truth, truth must necessarily precede error."[1]

Tertullian's "principle of time" is one of the main criteria modern historians use to evaluate conflicting historical accounts. The one written closest to the actual events is normally given credence over one written much later.

After all, how much confidence would you have in a New Testament manuscript that differed from others and yet was produced 1400 years after the apostles had died? Particularly if you had available a New Testament manuscript that was compiled within a few decades after the apostles had died? Why then do we choose *doctrines* that were first taught 1,400 years or more after the deaths of the apostles over ones that were taught within a few decades of their lives?

The Cumulative Effect
Of Small Changes

A copy of anything is rarely a perfect duplication of the original. As Christianity has been duplicated from generation to generation, it has undergone many changes. From generation to generation, most of these changes have been very small, almost imperceptible. However, the cumulative effect of small changes over hundreds of years can be significant. Take for example the English language. From generation to generation, our language changes very slowly. The change is so slow that we can barely discern any difference between the way we speak and the way our grandparents spoke, except for slang. However, over hundreds of years, the accumulation of these small changes is quite noticeable. For example, when we try to read thirteenth century medieval English, it's almost like trying to read a foreign language.

The same is true of Christianity. I'm sure that second century Christianity wasn't a perfect duplication of apostolic Christianity. But the second century Christians were basically only one generation away from the apostles. We're nineteen centuries away! How reasonable is it for us to argue that, after nineteen hundred years, evangelical Christianity is basically unchanged from that of the apostles? Particularly when, at the same time, we claim that orthodox Christianity had radically changed only 50 years after the apostles died?

The Advantages of Language
And Culture

But the element of time is not the only advantage that the early Christians had over us. They were also in a much better position to accurately interpret the apostles' writings.

To begin with, the early Christians could read the New Testament Scriptures in the original Greek of the apostles. How many of us can say the same? Our pastors have to study ancient Greek for several years as part of their seminary training. Yet very few of them can speak ancient Greek fluently. Most can't even read and comprehend a Greek text without the aid of a Greek-English lexicon. The early Christians, however, didn't have to study ancient Greek; it was their native language. They not only spoke in Greek, they *thought* in it.

How Much Do You Know About
Early Mediterranean Culture?

What about the culture barrier? Most Christians today know

extremely little about the cultural or historical setting in which the New Testament was written. As often as not, what today's Christians think they know is more myth than fact. Even scholars who devote their entire lives to studying the cultural and historical background of New Testament Christianity can never understand it as well as the people who lived in it. So once again the early Christians had an important advantage over us when it came to correctly interpreting the Scriptures.

Have You Ever Talked To The Apostle John?

Finally, the first generation of early Christians had the opportunity to hear the apostles *in person* and to ask them questions.

Clement of Rome is an example. He was a personal disciple of both Paul and Peter.[2] Paul specifically mentions Clement by name in his letter to the Philippians, saying, "I ask you, loyal yokefellow, help these women who have contended at my side in the cause of the gospel, along with Clement and the rest of my fellow workers, whose names are in the book of life." (Phil. 4:3) How likely is it that Clement, Paul's co-worker, misunderstood what Paul was teaching about salvation? Why would Paul have spoken so highly of Clement if he were teaching in error?

I've already mentioned Polycarp's relationship with the Apostle John, who appointed him overseer (bishop) of the church at Smyrna. If the angels of the seven churches in Revelation refer to the overseers of those churches, it's quite possible that Smyrna's "angel" was Polycarp. And, in Revelation, Jesus says nothing about the church in Smyrna teaching wrong doctrine. In fact, Jesus had no words of correction at all for the church of Smyrna (Rev. 2:8-11). Evidently, the church of Smyrna was on the right course under the leadership of Polycarp, or else Jesus would have stated otherwise.

But hearing the apostles explain their own writings wasn't simply a nicety, it was a necessity. After all, Peter himself commented about Paul's writings, "He writes the same way in all his letters, speaking in them of these matters. His letters contain some things that are *hard to understand*, which ignorant and unstable people distort" (2 Pet. 3:16). Peter was writing to Christians who spoke Greek fluently and who shared the same cultural setting as Paul. But even with those advantages, Peter admits that some things in Paul's writings were "hard to understand." Yet, we, who live nearly 2000 years later and speak a different language, act as though it were impossible that *we* may be misunderstanding his writings.

Unfortunately, Peter does not explain what the "ignorant and unstable people" were teaching. Were they, perhaps, interpreting Paul's writings the way we do? After all, the deceivers who were so widespread at the end of the first century were the gnostics. And as we've seen, their interpretation of Paul's letters were in many ways identical to ours.

The Primary Teaching of The Apostles Was Oral

All of Jesus' teaching was oral. He didn't leave even a single word of written instruction for the church. When the church was founded on the day of Pentecost, the only Christian teaching it had was oral. In fact, our New Testament wasn't completed until nearly the end of the first century. So the first century church relied largely on the oral teachings of the apostles, because the apostles primarily taught orally.

After all, do you really think that Paul, the tireless evangelist and teacher, had nothing more to share with the early church than the 13 or 14 brief letters in our New Testament? Of course not! Paul exhorted the Thessalonians, "So then, brothers, stand firm and hold to the teachings we passed on to you, whether by *word of mouth* or by letter" (2 Thess. 2:15). Paul wanted the

Thessalonians to adhere to his oral teachings just as much as to his written teachings.

What about the other apostles? Do you think that the sum total of Peter's teaching was merely seven pages of writing? Do you really think that the apostles Andrew, James, Philip, Bartholomew, Thomas, James (son of Alphaeus), Simon the Zealot, and Judas (son of James) had nothing whatsoever to share with the church? Preposterous! These were handpicked men who had spent three years of personal training in the close company of Jesus himself. The testimony of the early church is that all of the apostles were actively preaching and teaching the gospel.

Paul told the Corinthians, "Now, I praise you because you remember me in everything, and hold firmly to the *traditions, just as I delivered them to you*" (1 Cor. 11:2 NAS). Paul goes on, however, to rebuke some of the Corinthian women who were not wearing prayer coverings. Yet, there had been no prior written command from the apostles for a Christian woman to cover her head while praying or prophesying. But there was definitely an apostolic custom or tradition, as Paul testifies: "If anyone wants to be contentious about this, we have no other practice nor do the churches of God" (1 Cor. 11:16).

But please don't jump ahead of me. I'm not saying that there were any additional doctrines, moral commandments, or revelations that were handed down orally to the early Christians. In fact, the writings of the early Christians are the strongest evidence we have that there were none. Our New Testament contains everything essential for salvation.

Instead, apostolic tradition (the oral teaching of the apostles), had two primary funcions. The first was to establish ecclesiastical practices—such as, methods of worship, the mode of baptism, and church government. In fact, most of the practices of the first century church in these areas were matters of apostolic tradition or custom—not written direction. For example, nowhere in the New Testament are Christians told when they should meet together or how often they should observe communion. But the testimony of the early Christians shows that there were some very definite traditions that had been handed down by the apostles or their associates on these matters.

Church government itself was established by the oral teachings of the apostles. When Paul gave Timothy and Titus instructions about selecting elders and deacons, he was not instituting a new form of church government (1 Tim. 3:1-13; Titus 1:5-9). He was simply describing the type of men who should fill the positions of oversight that had already been implemented.

The second function of apostolic tradition was the clarification and enlargement of matters that were discussed (or that would later be discussed) in the New Testament writings. The apostles never intended that the church try to interpret their writings in a vacuum, apart from their extensive oral teachings. Because the early Christians clung to the wealth of apostolic oral instruction, they had an enormous advantage over us in interpreting the Scriptures.

Were The Early Christians Deliberately Falsifying The Truth?

But, of course, all I've shown is that the early Christians were in a *better position* than we to correctly understand and imitate the apostles. I haven't shown they didn't deliberately change the teachings handed down to them by the apostles. Did they do so? The answer may be crucial to our relationship with God.

12

Were The Teachings
Of The Apostles
Deliberately Altered?

If Christianity changed radically within a few decades after
the Apostle John's death, it wasn't because the church *misunderstood* the apostles' teachings. After all, if the very men who
were personally taught by the apostles couldn't understand
them, how can *anyone* hope to understand the apostles? No,
any dramatic departure from apostolic Christianity by the early
Christians would have been deliberate.

They Believed There Was
No New Special Revelation

Did the early Christians think the apostles were in error on
some matters? Did they believe the church had new revelation
after the apostles or that some apostolic teaching was outdated?

The answer to these questions is an unequivocal "No!" The
early church specifically taught that there was no special
doctrinal revelation beyond the apostles and that everything we
need to know about God had been revealed to the apostles.
Further, the church believed that the apostles taught nothing in
error and that their teachings applied to Christians in all ages.

For example, Tertullian wrote, "In the Lord's apostles we possess our authority. Even they did not of themselves choose to introduce anything [new], but they faithfully delivered to the nations (of mankind) the doctrine they had received from Christ. If, therefore, even 'an angel from heaven should preach any other gospel,' we would call him accursed.... We therefore draw up this rule: Since the Lord Jesus Christ sent the apostles to preach, no others should be received as preachers [of original doctrine] than those whom Christ appointed.... The Son did not reveal His Father to any other than the apostles, whom He sent forth to preach these things He revealed to them."[1]

In fact, the primary confrontation between the early church and the early heretical groups was over the issue of revelation. Nearly all the heretics claimed to have new revelation beyond the teachings of the apostles. Irenaeus, the pupil of Polycarp, declared on behalf of the church: "The Lord of all gave to His apostles the power of the Gospel, through whom we have known the truth.... It is unlawful to claim that [the apostles] preached before they possessed 'perfect knowledge,' as some [gnostics] venture to say, boasting themselves as improvers of the apostles."[2]

The early church was unwavering in its position that there was no special revelation after the apostles. Therefore, the church summarily rejected any teaching or doctrine that hadn't been heard from the lips of the apostles.

The Early Church Leaders Were Men Of Integrity

But, of course, simply because the early Christians *said* there was no new revelation after the apostles, doesn't prove they weren't wickedly altering the apostles' teachings anyway. What about their *integrity*? Were the early Christian leaders princi-pled men of God or were they unscrupulous seekers of wealth and power? The overwhelming evidence is that they were humble, honest men of God. For one thing, the early Christian leaders didn't profit materially from their positions. As I've already discussed, early church leaders were not paid a salary. Serving as a presbyter in the early church usually meant giving up material comforts to live in poverty. Only the heretics profited financially from their positions of leadership. There was little to attract a person to church leadership other than an honest desire to serve God.

Moreover, during times of persecution, church leaders were specially targeted by soldiers and mobs. In some periods, being appointed as an overseer was tantamount to receiving a death sentence. Yet, almost without exception, the leaders of the early church willingly endured inhuman tortures rather than to deny Christ. A substantial number of the Christian leaders cited in this book—Ignatius, Polycarp, Justin Martyr, Hippolytus, Cyprian, Methodius, and Origen—willingly died for their faith in Christ. If these men had been dishonestly twisting the teachings of Jesus and his apostles, would they have been willing to die for Jesus? The gnostics certainly were not. Although claiming to have special revelation from God, they were all too ready to deny Jesus when faced with torture and death. Few people will die for something they know is a deliberate lie.

Don't we point out this very fact when defending the truthfulness of Jesus' resurrection? Don't we argue that the apostles wouldn't have willingly died for what they knew was a lie? Would the pupils of the apostles have done any differently?

They Assembled And Preserved
Our New Testament

Actually, the authenticity of the New Testament itself is intertwined with the integrity of the early Christians. After all, it was the early church leaders who collected, preserved, and tested the genuineness of the writings we now call the New Testament.

Some Christians have the mistaken impression that at the close of the apostolic age the apostles handed the church a bound collection of writings called "the New Testament," telling the church that everything it needed to know was contained in those writings. But that's not what happened. The various letters and narrative accounts written by the apostles and other disciples were actually collected separately by the early Christian congregations. The apostles never told the church which writings to accept and which to reject. With the guidance of the Holy Spirit, the early Christians had to decide for themselves which writings were genuinely from the apostles and which were not—which was no easy task.

For one thing, numerous spurious gospels and "apostolic" letters were circulating. In fact, there were more fake accounts of the life of Jesus and the acts of the apostles than there were genuine ones. Have you ever heard of the Gospel of Thomas? What about the Gospel of Nicodemus? Or the Acts of Philip or the Acts of Andrew and Matthias? Have you ever read the Revelation of Paul? Probably not. The reason is that the early church did not accept those writings as genuine.

If the church had wanted to depart from the teachings of the apostles, all it had to do was to accept some of those spurious books and reject some of the genuine apostolic writings. Or the church could have simply altered the genuine apostolic writings to make them fit the teachings of the church. Nobody would have called the church's hand on this, since everybody else outside the church was already doing these very things.

This leaves us between a rock and a hard place. If we say that the early Christian leaders were dishonest men who deliberately altered the *teachings* of the apostles, we have to admit the likelihood that they would have also dishonestly altered their *writings*. In fact, when we defend the veracity and authenticity of the New Testament writings to skeptics, we invariably cite the use and testimony of the early Christians as one of our main bases of authority.

The integrity of these men is particularly noticeable in their decisions on which books to include in the New Testament canon. For example, knowing the early Christian doctrine of salvation and works, we would naturally expect to find that the early church placed great emphasis on the Letter of James and accepted its canonicity without question, while resisting the Letter to the Romans. But just the opposite is true. The early Christians rarely quoted from James, and many churches questioned its authenticity.[3] In contrast, they quoted abundantly from Paul, and they included his letters in the New Testament canon without hesitation.

What incredible integrity! They questioned the authenticity of the very book that most strongly supported their doctrinal beliefs on salvation. At the same time, they accepted without hesitation those books that might be interpreted as contradicting their beliefs. Would we have such integrity?

I don't see this type of integrity in the man from whom so many of our evangelical doctrines stem—Martin Luther. One of Luther's noteworthy accomplishments was his translation of the Bible into German. But his translation contained prefaces to each Bible book that steered the reader's attention away from parts of the Bible that didn't fit Luther's theology.

For example, in his preface to the New Testament, Luther wrote:

□ □ □ □ □ □ □ □ □ □

"It would be right and proper that this book should appear without preface and without any other name than that of its authors, and convey only its own name and its own language. But many wild interpretations and prefaces have driven the thought of Christians to a point where no one any longer knows what is Gospel or Law, Old Testament or

New. Necessity demands, therefore, that it should have an announcement, or preface, by which the simple man can be brought back from the old notions to the right road, and be taught what he is to expect in this book, so that he may not seek laws and commandments where he ought to be seeking the Gospel and God's promises....

"If I had to do without one or the other—either the works or preaching of Christ—I would rather do without His works than His preaching. For the works do not help me, but His words give life, as He Himself says. Now John writes very little about the works of Christ, but very much about His preaching. But the other Evangelists write much of His works and little of His preaching. Therefore John's Gospel is the one, tender, true chief Gospel, *far, far to be preferred to the other three* and placed high above them. So, too, the Epistles of St. Paul and St. Peter far surpass the other three Gospels—Matthew, Mark and Luke.

"In a word, St. John's Gospel and his first Epistle, St. Paul's Epistles, especially Romans, Galatians, and Ephesians, and St. Peter's first Epistle are the books that show you Christ and teach you all that it is necessary and good for you to know, even though you were never to see or hear any other book or doctrine. Therefore *St. James' Epistle is really an epistle of straw*, compared to them; for it has nothing of the nature of the Gospel about it."[4]

□ □ □ □ □ □ □ □ □ □

Luther claimed that the only reason he preferred the Gospel of John over the other three gospels was that it contained more of Jesus' preaching. But that isn't true. The Gospel of Matthew contains nearly *twice* as much of Jesus' preaching as the Gospel of John.

A person doesn't need to be very perceptive to see what Luther's real motive was. The Bible books Luther disparaged happen to be the very books that indicate that obedience is necessary for salvation. For example, in Matthew we find such sayings as "Not everyone who says to me 'Lord, Lord,' will enter the kingdom of heaven, but only he who does the will of my Father" (Matt. 7:21); and "he who stands firm to the end will be saved" (Matt. 24:13). James tells us that "a person is justified by what he does and not by faith alone" (Jas. 2:24). Luther was willing to stoop to disparaging the Word of God just to advance his own theology. It is no wonder that most of modern, liberal theology began in Lutheran seminaries.

In short, I see a sharp contrast between the integrity of the early Christians and that of the founder of the Reformation. How much confidence could we have in the New Testament canon if it had been compiled by Luther rather than by the early churches? At the same time, how much confidence can we have in our evangelical doctrines that came from Luther?

The Early Christians Were Ultra-Conservative

The early Christians were ultra-conservative, equating change with error. Since they expected no new revelation after the apostles, they summarily rejected any new teachings that had not come from the apostles. For example, one early congregation made the following comment in a letter to another congregation: "You well understand, no doubt, that those who seek to set up any new doctrines have the habit of very readily perverting any proofs they desire to take from the Scriptures to conform to their own notions.... Consequently, a disciple of Christ ought to receive nothing new as doctrine that is in addition to what has been once committed to us by the apostles."[5]

When change is equated with error, things do not change very quickly. A comparison of the writings of the second-century church with those of the third-century church, demonstrates that there were very few changes in doctrines or moral precepts between those two centuries. Oh, there were some minor changes, but these related primarily to church government and discipline.[6]

They Consulted The Disciples
Of The Apostles

Another thing that impressed me about the early Christian leaders was their sincere desire to avoid accidentally straying from the practices of the apostles. As I've mentioned, the first century churches clung to the oral tradition of the apostles, and they consulted with the apostles when questions arose. If the apostles weren't available, they consulted with leaders in those churches where some of the apostles had personally taught. This latter practice continued up until the time of Constantine. For example, Irenaeus wrote, "Suppose a dispute arises relative to some important question among us. Should we not have recourse to the most ancient churches with whom the apostles had constant dealings and learn from them what is certain and clear in regard to the question?"[7]

Remember, as late as 150 there were still elders in the church who had been personally taught by one or more apostles. Well into the third century, there were still church leaders who had been taught by one or more disciples of an apostle. Of course, consulting with apostolically founded churches was not as good as talking with the apostles themselves. But considering the ultra-conservative spirit of the early church, this was a valid method to keep from straying from the practices and teachings of the apostles.

You should note that this practice was entirely voluntary. No church had ecclesiastical authority over other churches. Also, remember that the rationale for this practice was *not* that the apostolic churches had any present authority or revelation from God, but that they had the best link to past revelation.

They All Taught The Same
Basic Doctrines

As I've previously mentioned, early Christianity was marked by a diversity of thought on the finer points of doctrine. At the same time, most of the basic beliefs and practices—including the ones discussed in this book—were nearly universally taught throughout the early church. This universality of basic beliefs convinces me that these beliefs must have come from the apostles. That's because there was no second-century Christian of church-wide influence who could have originated them.

In fact, Tertullian pointed this out to the gnostics and other heretics who claimed that the church wasn't correctly teaching the doctrines of the apostles. Tertullian's defense to this charge might just as well be addressed to Christians today:

◻ ◻ ◻ ◻ ◻ ◻ ◻ ◻ ◻ ◻

"It is absurd to claim that the apostles either were ignorant of the whole scope of the message they were given to declare or that they failed to teach the entire rule of faith. Let us see if perhaps the churches, through their own fault, altered the faith delivered to them by the apostles.... Suppose, then, that all of the churches have erred and that the Holy Spirit did not have enough concern for even one church to lead it into truth, even though that is the reason Christ sent Him to us.... Suppose, too, that the Holy Spirit, the Steward of God and Vicar of Christ, neglected His office and permitted the churches to understand incorrectly and to teach differently than what He Himself was teaching through the apostles.

"If that is the case, is it likely that so many churches would have gone astray and all still end up with one and the same faith? No random deviation by so many people could result in all of them coming to the same conclusion. If the churches had fallen into doctrinal errors, they would have certainly ended up with varying teachings. However, when that which was deposited [i.e., the Christian faith] among many is still found to be one and the same, it is not the result of error, but of long established custom."[8]

□ □ □ □ □ □ □ □ □ □ □

I find it rather difficult to circumvent Tertullian's argument. If the churches had departed from the one true faith preached by the apostles, how did they all end up teaching the same thing? There were no church-wide councils, seminaries, printed literature, or any other means to quickly disseminate erroneous teachings throughout the church. So how could all the congregations have independently come up with the same interpretations and practices unless they were simply following what Paul and the other apostles had taught as they visited the congregations during their travels? In fact, even three hundred years after the death of Jesus, orthodox Christians were still one united body. Yet, three hundred years after the Reformation, Protestant or evangelical Christians were divided into hundreds of dissenting groups and sects. Shouldn't this tell us something?

They Walked In The Footsteps Of Jesus

A friend who heard I was studying the early Christian writings made the following comment to me in a letter, "I have a theory. The way to determine the authenticity of those who are regarded as 'church fathers' is to compare their ideas and way of life with those reflected in the life of Jesus and his disciples." I realized, of course, that he was right. It would be difficult to maintain that the early Christians were upholding apostolic teachings if their practices and lifestyle contradicted the very things that Jesus and his apostles taught.

But as we've already seen, the early Christians lived *very literally* by the teachings of Jesus and the apostles. Their lives reflected their loyalty to Jesus.

What Did Jesus Say About Their Doctrines?

Finally, and most importantly, we have the direct testimony of Jesus himself. At the close of the first century, he evaluated seven representative churches and gave his analysis of them in the Revelation to John. Only a few years separated this Revelation of John from the earliest writings I've discussed in this book, such as the letters of Ignatius and Clement of Rome.

In Revelation, what did Jesus have to say to those seven representative churches? Did he reprimand them for teaching false doctrines? Did he rebuke them for believing that works play a role in salvation? No, just the opposite.

He exhorted them to *increase* their works. He told the church in Sardis that their works were not complete. But He said nothing to any of them about their doctrinal beliefs. In fact, he encouraged a couple of the churches to hold firmly to what they had. (Rev. 2 and 3). His primary criticism to several of the churches was that they tolerated idolatry and immorality, a problem that was remedied by the second century church.

There is nothing in Jesus' messages to indicate that any of the seven churches were teaching false theology. In fact, as I've mentioned before, Jesus had no rebuke whatsoever for the church in Smyrna, where Polycarp was the overseer or bishop. What better stamp of approval could a church possibly have that its teachings and practices were pleasing to God?

But if the early Christians didn't change the teachings of the apostles, who did?

13

What Happened To Early Christianity?

It has been said that "patriotism is the last refuge of a scoundrel."[1] In Christianity, theology is the last refuge of a spiritually weak church. Bare theology requires no faith, no love, and no sacrifice. A faithless "Christian" who has no real relationship with God can give mental assent to a list of doctrines, the same as can the spiritually strongest Christian.

As persecution of the early church lessened towards the end of the third century, and as the church grew bigger and stronger, it became spiritually weaker. And, as it became weaker, it began to place greater emphasis on theological doctrines and less emphasis on lifestyle. By the end of the third century, after an extended period without persecution, bickering between congregations over doctrinal issues had become fairly widespread.

The church historian Eusebius, who lived during this period, records the sad situation that had developed: "On account of the abundant freedom [granted by the government], we fell into laxity and sloth. We envied and reviled each other, and were almost, as it were, taking up arms against one another, leaders assailing leaders with words like spears, and people forming parties against people."[2] Even though the church remained one, undivided body, there was friction between churches and

118

between individuals. As a result, the church was spiritually unprepared for the tidal wave of savage persecution that engulfed it at the beginning of the fourth century.

How Constantine Tried To "Christianize" The Empire

Ever since the time of Nero in the first century, there had been no continuing dynasty of Roman emperors. Instead, an emperor usually reigned only a short while before he was overthrown by a rival claimant to the throne. In A.D. 306, several rivals shared the ruling power of the Roman Empire. Severus ruled Italy and North Africa, and Constantine ruled Britain and Gaul. Two other men ruled the eastern empire. When Severus was dethroned by a rival named Maxentius, Constantine declared himself to be the sole legitimate emperor of the western Roman Empire.

Constantine was a born leader—a decisive man of action who could both inspire and organize people. Soon after declaring himself to be the sole emperor of the West, he began a slow march across the Alps to Rome to dethrone Maxentius. After a string of victories, Constantine began the final leg of his march on Rome in 312. During that march to Rome, he had an experience that was to have a profound impact on world history and on the course of Christianity.

Eusebius, the church historian, later described what Constantine told him had happened: "He said that about noon, when the day was already beginning to decline, he saw with his own eyes the sign of a cross of light in the heavens above the sun, bearing the inscription, 'By this, conquer.'"[3] Constantine said he later had a dream in which Christ told him to construct a military standard in the form of a cross. This standard would protect him in all battles with his enemies. As a result of these experiences, Constantine ordered a special military standard to be constructed. It consisted of a gold-plated spear placed upright, transversed by a shorter bar—forming the shape of a cross. A gold wreath, studded with jewels, was laid over the crossbar, and the initials of Christ were placed inside the wreath.

Carrying this standard into battle, the armies of Constantine decisively defeated those of Maxentius at the Milvian Bridge, about two miles outside the walls of Rome. Constantine became the sole ruler of the western empire, and he credited his victory to the God of the Christians.

Constantine's subsequent relationship to the church can only be understood in light of the relationship that Roman emperors had always had with the religion of their subjects. The Romans were very religious, and they attributed their success and prosperity to the gods who had blessed them. Religion in the Roman Empire was a *public* matter, and religion and state had always been closely intertwined. Invocations and sacrifices were made to the gods during public ceremonies, and public worship of the gods was considered a matter of *patriotic* duty. To offend the gods was a crime against the state.[4]

Apparently, Constantine genuinely believed that the God of the Christians had given him his victory. He also believed this same God would now protect the Roman Empire as long as the emperors worshiped Him and the church was faithful to Him. So Constantine began showering blessings on the church and its leaders. In conjunction with the eastern emperor, he issued the Edict of Milan in 313, which said in part: "[We resolve] to grant both to the Christians and to all men freedom to follow the religion which they choose, so that whatever heavenly divinity exists may be favorably inclined to us and to all who live under our government."[5]

Notice that Constantine did not make Christianity the state religion of the Roman Empire. He simply gave Christianity legal recognition for the first time, putting it on an equal footing with all other religions in the empire. Nevertheless, Christianity was now the religion of the emperor himself, which gave it prestige over all the pagan religions. Many church buildings had been destroyed in the persecution that preceded Constantine's enthronement. So Constantine rebuilt most of these church buildings at public expense. He also began paying salaries out of the state treasury to the bishops and presbyters of most congregations. He passed laws specifically exempting church leaders from any obligatory state service.

Constantine did this to enable the bishops and presbyters to devote their full time and energy to their congregations. He believed that a spiritually healthy church would ensure God's continuing favor on the empire.[6] Constantine also promoted Christians to positions of prominence in the state and surrounded himself with Christian advisors. He even had Christian bishops accompany his troops into battle to ensure God's favor.[7]

How Friendship With The World Ruined The Church

The church was now like a naive young girl who suddenly had been swept off of her feet by a rival suitor. The world wanted to be friends with the church, and the church saw no harm in reciprocating. For the first time in history, it was *socially prestigious* to be a Christian. Preference was given to Christians in appointments to state offices.

However, the world's friendship had a disastrous effect on the church. As Constantine began passing laws to "Christianize" Roman society, the distinction between Christians and non-Christians became blurred. In the past, there had been little to attract anyone to the church other than a genuine faith in God. Fair-weather converts were ferreted out as soon as it came time to carry their crosses. Unregenerate persons in the church were a small minority. But now that Christianity was socially rewarding, people began flocking into the church in hordes. Already spiritually weak, the church was simply unable to assimilate such a large mass of new "converts." Before long, the name "Christian" no longer stood for a holy lifestyle. It merely indicated that a person gave mental assent to a particular creed and that he had partaken of the various Christian rites, such as baptism.

One of the immediate effects of the church's friendship with the world was that it began adopting the world's methods. This was inevitable, because the world can't do things God's way. To do things God's way requires God's power. And mobs of unregenerate people using the name "Christian" don't have God's power. Nor do they even *want* to do things God's way, since God's way requires patience, willingness to suffer, and absolute trust in Him.

We Dare You To Persecute Us!

At first, the innovative methods of the world seemed more effective than the old ways of doing things. For example, the church changed its method of coping with persecution and government oppression. In the past, Christians had simply tried to hide or flee from persecution. They refused to physically fight their persecutors or retaliate against them. However, the crowds of unregenerate persons who had bloated the church weren't about to meekly accept death, torture, or oppression.

For example, when Constantine's son sent one of his generals to Constantinople to depose the church's bishop, the congregation formed a mob. That night when the general was asleep, the mob set his lodging house on fire. When he finally ran out of the house, dazed and coughing from the smoke, they pounced on him. Then they dragged him through the cobble-stone streets of the city and savagely beat him to death.[8] This was no isolated case; it was now the *normal* response of the church to governmental oppression. The character of Christianity had changed.

Silencing Heretics

The world also had a different means of handling heretics. Constantine reasoned that the church would be much healthier if there were no heretics around to mislead people. So he used his power to try to eradicate heresy, issuing the following edict:

> Understand now, by this present statute, you Novatians, Valentinians, Marcionites, Paulicians, and Montanists, and all the rest of you who devise and support heresies by means of your private assemblies ... that your offenses are so hateful and altogether atrocious that a single day would be insufficient to recount them all.... Since it is no longer possible to tolerate your deadly errors, we hereby give you warning that none of you are to meet together hereafter. We have therefore ordered that your meeting places be taken from you. And you are expressly forbidden to hold your superstitious and senseless meetings, not only in public, but also in private homes, or any other place.[9]

Only a few decades previously it had been a crime to be a Christian. Now it was a crime to be a *heretic.* Most of the church silently accepted this development without protest. How much easier it was to silence heretics through the power of the state than to argue with them.

But soon large segments of the church were labeling each other as heretics and using the arm of the state against each other. Sadly to say, when the Muslim armies invaded Egypt in 639, most Christians in Egypt welcomed them as liberators, for they fared better at the hands of the Muslims than they did at the hands of their fellow Christians.

The Wedding Feast And The Dragnet

Once the church opened itself to change, how could it know whether God approved the changes? Many thought the answer was easy. To them, growth indicated God's approval. Christianity had grown rapidly in the first three centuries, but after the conversion of Constantine the church *mushroomed.* At the time of the Edict of Milan (313 A.D.), probably about a tenth of the Roman Empire had converted to Christianity. But that had taken nearly three hundred years. In less than a hundred years after the Edict of Milan, nearly all of the other 90 percent had been "converted." Many in the church believed that this rapid growth was a sure sign of God's approval. But it wasn't.

Instead, what was happening was the fulfillment of Jesus' parable about the wedding feast:

> The kingdom of heaven may be compared to a king, who gave a wedding feast for his son....Then he said to his slaves,...."Go therefore to the main highways, and as many as you find there, invite to the wedding feast." And those slaves went out into the streets, and gathered together all they found, both evil and good; and the wedding hall was filled with dinner guests. But when the king came in to look over the dinner guests, he saw there a man not dressed in wedding clothes, and he said to him, "Friend, how did you come in here without wedding clothes?" And he was speechless. Then the king said to the servants, "Bind him hand and foot, and cast him into the outer darkness; in that place there will be weeping and gnashing of teeth." For many are called, but few are chosen (Matt. 22:2,8-14 NAS).

Now that Christianity was fashionable, everyone was flocking into the church, "both evil and good." Yet, as Jesus had said, only a few of those called would be chosen.

Again, Jesus prophetically described the post-Constantinian church in His parable of the dragnet: "The kingdom of heaven is like a dragnet cast into the sea, and gathering fish of every kind; and when it was filled, they drew it up on the beach; and they sat down, and gathered the good fish into containers, but the bad they threw away. So it will be at the end of the age; the angels shall come forth and take out the wicked *from among the righteous*, and will cast them into the furnace of fire" (Matt. 13:47-50).

Although this parable applies to the church in all ages, it was particularly descriptive of the church after the conversion of Constantine. The dragnet was now indiscriminately bringing in clean and unclean fish alike.

Yet, the church itself never disappeared. Jesus had prophesied that His church would be built on the rock, and the gates of Hades would not prevail against it. The torch of early Christianity—the way of the cross—has continued through the centuries. But that torch has been carried by the few, not the many.

14

The Myth Of
The Pilgrim Church

Most denominations, sects, and cults today purport to be able to trace their lineage all the way back to the apostles. That's because they instinctively recognize that the true church must be able to trace itself all the way back to the apostles. So no matter what group we belong to, regardless of how recently our denomination was formed, we all try to find a way to trace our church back to the first century. Usually, we attempt to do this through the various sects and schismatic groups through history that are commonly called the "pilgrim church" or the "trail of blood."

I have always tried to trace my doctrinal views through that same chain. So when I began to study church history in earnest, I naturally expected to find historical verification for this "pilgrim church." Yet, after considerable research, I realized that once again I had been misled. The pilgrim church never existed. Oh, there were dozens of sects and schismatic groups throughout history, such as the Montanists, Novatianists, Paulicians, Priscillians, Albigenses, Lollards, and Waldensians. But those groups didn't even believe alike. There was no continuation—either physically or spiritually—from one group to the other. In fact, many of these groups existed at the same time, but wanted nothing to do with each other.

More importantly, those groups didn't believe the same things as do the modern churches and cults that claim them as ancestors. If most of those early groups were still around today, they would be called heretics by the very churches and cults who pretend to be their descendants. For example, the Manicheans, Paulicians, Bogomils, Cathars and Albigenses were all gnostics. They taught that an evil deity created the earth and that he was the God of the Old Testament. Many of those groups forbade marriage and condemned the eating of meat (1 Tim. 4:3).

Not one single one of the pre-Reformation groups—from the Montanists to the Waldensians—taught the modern evangelical view of salvation by faith alone. Quite a few of them, such as the Montanists, Novatianists, Donatists, Lollards, and Waldensians, strongly maintained that living by the Sermon on the Mount was necessary for salvation.

One of the dead give-aways that the existence of this "pilgrim church" is a myth is the fact that Baptists, Jehovah's Witnesses, Church of Christ, Seventh Day Adventists, Mennonites, Pentecostals, and hundreds of other widely-varying denominations and cults all basically claim the same past groups as their ancestors. Obviously, for such varied denominations and sects to profess the same lineage, they have had to be very sloppy or dishonest in their historical research. I think the truth of the matter is that we would rather hold to a mythical lineage than to face a truth we don't want to admit.

The Real Trail Of Early Christianity

As I have said, the existence of the "pilgrim church"—as a chain of separate schismatic groups—is a myth. However, there has been a genuine pilgrim church through the ages *within* the visible body of professing Christians. This pilgrim church preserved a very real trail of early Christianity through the ages. The spirit of early Christianity did not die with Constantine.

From the very beginning of Christianity, there had always been godly believers who didn't compromise with the world—even when the church in their area did. For example, Jesus told the church in Sardis, "I know your deeds, that you have a name that you are alive, but you are dead." Yet, he went on to say, "But you have a few people in Sardis who have not soiled their garments; and they will walk with Me in white, for they are worthy" (Rev. 3:1,4).

Some committed Christians through the centuries married and raised godly families of believers. Others made a decision to become "eunuchs for the Kingdom of heaven" (Matt. 19:12). That is, they either never married or else they remained single after being widowed. Commonly, those unmarried Christians lived together with other single Christians of the same sex and devoted their lives to prayer and ministry. That was the informal beginning of what are now known as religious orders or societies.

Actually, it was the apostles themselves who authorized the formation of the first religious order—the order of widows Paul wrote:

> "To be on the church's roll of widows, a widow should be not less than sixty years of age. She must have been married only once. Her good character will be attested to by her good deeds. Has she brought up children? Has she been hospitable to strangers? Has she washed the feet of Christian visitors? Has she given help to those in distress? In a word, has she been eager to do every possible good work?
>
> "Refuse to enroll the younger widows, for when their passions estrange them from Christ they will want to marry. This will bring them condemnation for breaking their first pledge" (1 Tim. 5:9-13 NAB).

The early Christian writings attest that the order of widows in the early church carried on active ministries of intercessory prayer and visitation of sick and imprisoned Christians. Informal orders of virgins carried on similar ministries.

As the church became increasingly worldly after Constantine's reign, more and more Christians chose the way of asceticism or monasticism as a way to avoid being sucked into the worldliness around them. The first ones to follow this way of life generally retreated into the desert as solitary individuals or couples. Later, entire communities of such committed Christians began to flourish. Although these spiritual communities and societies were initially composed of only celibate men or women, in the west some of the religious orders began to accept "tertiary" members. "Tertiaries" were single or married persons who maintained a life of separation from the world although living among everyday people. Each community or society lived by a Rule of Life, as had the Nazarites and Rechabites of old. Among other things, each community's Rule of Life prescribed regular times of prayer, worship, physical labor, and Bible reading. Perhaps the most famous Rule of Life drawn up for these spiritual communities was that of Benedict (c. 500). His Rule still governs life in many monasteries and spiritual societies to this day.

Generally speaking, the members of these spiritual orders and communities continued to live the separated, holy lifestyle that once was the *normal* lifestyle of all Christians. That is not to say that there were no godly people who lived outside of these communities. Indeed, there were many. Nor is it to say that all those who lived in religious communities were necessarily godly men and women. The communities certainly had their share of hypocrites and godless people. In fact, by the late Middle Ages, the spiritual state of many religious communities in the west had become scandalous.

Still, the vast majority of great spiritual figures through the centuries from Constantine until the Reformation were members of some type of religious order or community, or else they lived as ascetics. I'm speaking of such noted Christians as Basil, Augustine, John Chyrsostom, Patrick of Ireland, Columba, Benedict, Bernard of Clairvaux, Julian of Norwich, Dominic, Savonarola, and Thomas à Kempis.

The person who is perhaps the most-admired figure in all of western Christianity was himself a monk—Francis of Assisi. Catholic, Protestant, evangelical, and even secular historians have all been touched by the life of simplicity and godliness lived by Francis and his initial followers. As one Protestant historian expressed it, "Francis sought no positions of honor nor a place with the great. With simple mind, he sought to serve his fellowmen by republishing the precepts of the Gospel, and living them out in his own example....Few men of history have made so profound an impression as did Francis. His personality shed light far and near in his own time. But his mission extends to all the centuries....He is at home in all ages by reason of his Apostolic simplicity and his artless gentleness."[1]

Monasticism and religious communities especially flowered in the ancient Celtic Church in Britain and Ireland. Not only did the Celtic monks convert the barbarian tribes that inhabited much of Britain, but they also carried on extensive evangelism throughout continental Europe and into Africa. In the Far East, Christian monks from Persia took Christianity into China by the seventh century, and eventually reached Japan, Korea, and Vietnam. In the ninth century, two Christian monks, Cyril and Methodius, brought Christianity to the Slavic peoples of eastern Europe.

Many monks, nuns, and spiritual communities were at the forefront of carrying the torch of the early Christian lifestyle through the centuries. They also served as the primary evangelists of Christianity for many centuries. Unfortunately, they generally did little or nothing to effectuate doctrinal reform when it was needed. Nevertheless, it was a monk—Martin Luther—who lit the spark that touched off the Reformation.

15

Was The Reformation A Return To Early Christianity?

The issue that sparked the Reformation was the Roman Catholic practice of granting indulgences. In Roman Catholic theology, an indulgence is the remission of the temporal penalty of sin. Roman Catholics believe that the Pope has authority to grant such indulgences to shorten the length of time a person spends in purgatory. The whole theology of indulgences is built around three Roman Catholic doctrines that were unknown to the early church:

- That most Christians go to purgatory when they die, where they suffer for a time in the purifying flames of purgatory before going on to heaven.

- That in heaven there is an inexhaustible treasury of excess merits from Christ, Mary, and the saints, which can be distributed to the faithful for full or partial remission of the temporal punishment due to sin.

- That the Pope is the treasurer of this infinite store of merits, and he can distribute these merits to those in the church as he deems appropriate.

In the early sixteenth century, the Pope needed funds to rebuild St. Peter's Church in Rome. So he authorized a preacher named Tetzel to raise contributions for this building. Those who contributed towards the rebuilding of St. Peter's would be granted an indulgence. Tetzel was an enthusiastic orator, and he travelled throughout Germany making all sorts of fantastic claims about what the "purchase" of an indulgence could accomplish. He played upon people's concerns for departed loved ones by preaching, "No sooner do the coins clink in the money chest than the soul of a loved one flies out of purgatory."[1]

One day a young man asked Tetzel if the purchase of an indulgence could obtain pardon for *any* sin. "Absolutely!" responded Tetzel. "What if the sin hasn't yet been committed, but is being contemplated by a person?" the man asked. "It makes no difference," Tetzel assured him. "No sin is too great."

With that, the young man eagerly purchased the indulgence. After Tetzel had completed his rather lucrative session in that village, he packed up his bags and journeyed toward the next town. On the way, he was confronted by a band of thieves who robbed him of all he had, including the money from that day's sale of indulgences. The grinning leader of the thieves was none other than the young man who had purchased an indulgence that afternoon in contemplation of a future sin—robbery.

Tetzel's fantastic claims didn't go unchecked. An energetic monk named Martin Luther, hot with righteous indignation, boldly confronted Tetzel and denounced his ludicrous claims. When the church did nothing to muzzle Tetzel, Luther nailed 95 theses to the door of the church in Wittenberg, proposing a public debate over the question of indulgences. Many Christians have misconceptions about these 95 theses. They weren't a list of Reformation doctrines, just a list of assertions concerning indulgences.

The flames of what may have otherwise been a rather small local dispute were fanned across all of Europe by a recent invention—the printing press. Without Luther's knowledge, his 95 theses were copied by local printers and circulated throughout most of Europe.

Soon a confrontation of major proportions began to grow. To solidify his doctrinal position against the extremes of Tetzel, Luther succumbed to what I call "Newton's Law of Theology."

Newton's Law of Theology

Sir Isaac Newton observed that, in physics, for every action there is an equal and opposite reaction. Sadly to say, Newton's law seems to apply as much to theology as it does to physics. For every heretic who moves away from true doctrine in one direction, there is a well-meaning "defender of the faith" who tries to defend orthodoxy by going to an equal and opposite extreme. Unfortunately, the "defender of the faith" often pulls much of the church with him in his over-reaction. The end result is that the heretic succeeds in adulterating the church, but in the opposite way from what he started out.

The Reformation is a classic example of this principle. The Roman Catholic Church clearly stood in need of reform. It had strayed in many areas from the pure apostolic teaching of the early church. It could no longer rightfully claim for itself the designation "catholic." That's because the word *catholic* means universal. Genuine catholic doctrines are the teachings that were believed by the whole undivided primitive church, at all times, throughout the entire world. Many of the teachings of the Roman Catholic Church cannot meet that criteria of true catholicity.

One of the unfortunate consequences of the Reformation is that most Bible-believing evangelicals and Protestants abhor the word "catholic." Actually, we should all *want* to be catholic. That is, we should want to hold to the teachings and practices of the early, apostolic, undivided church. What we don't want to necessarily be is *Roman.*

What the western church needed at the beginning of the sixteenth century was a humble, reasonable man of God who could wisely lead the church down the right path of reformation. It needed someone who could calmly and cautiously separate the *Roman* chaff from the original apostolic, *catholic* wheat. To do this, such a man would need to be thoroughly familiar with the writings and teachings of the early, undivided church.

But Martin Luther was not that kind of man. To be sure, he was a devout man of faith with enormous courage. Yet, he was also impulsive, hot-headed, and egotistical. Following "Newton's Law of Theology," he over-reacted to the errors of the Roman Catholic Church, throwing out, not only many Roman-made doctrines, but also many of the apostolic teachings of the early church. And in some instances, he actually held on to *Roman* doctrines and discarded truly *catholic* (apostolic) doctrines. In fact, rather than returning to the apostolic teachings of the early, pre-Constantinian church, Luther instead returned to the teachings of Augustine.

The Influence Of Augustine

Augustine, fourth century bishop of Hippo, has been one of the most influential Christian teachers of all time in the Western church. His influence on the Western church has rivalled that of the apostles themselves. That's because much of the Western church has read the apostles through his eyes. In fact, Augustine is almost universally recognized as *the* father of Western theology.

It is not without reason that Augustine's influence on Western theology has been so tremendous. Before becoming a Christian, he had been a teacher of persuasive argumentation and writing. As a bishop, he made use of these skills. Nobody in the Western church could successfully resist his argumentation. In his own lifetime, he became *the* theological authority in the West on practically every question of doctrine and morality.

Augustine was a sincere, godly man whose only aim was to help strengthen the church and to defend it against the heretical darts assailing it from all directions. Yet, again and again, he succumbed to "Newton's Law of Theology," over-reacting against the errors of various heretics. To answer Pelagius, he introduced the doctrine of absolute, double predestination. To counter the Arians, Augustine developed a doctrine of the Trinity that has ever since divided the Western church from both the Eastern church and the early church.

Some of the novel teachings he introduced that were unknown to the early church were:

- War can be holy.[2]

- Some of the practices and teachings of the apostles no longer apply to Christians because the apostles lived in a different age.[3]

- Unbaptized infants are eternally damned.[4]

- As a result of Adam's fall, man is totally depraved. He is absolutely unable to do anything good or to save himself. In fact, he's even unable to believe or have faith in God.[5]

- Therefore, humans can believe in God or have faith in Him *only* if by grace God first gives them this faith or belief. Man has no free will to choose either to believe or not to believe.[6]

- God's decision to save one person and condemn another, to give faith to one person and withhold it from another, is totally arbitrary. There's nothing we can do to influence God's choice. Before the creation of the world, God arbitrarily predestined (not simply foreknew) who would be saved and who would be damned. There's nothing we can do either in this life or the next to change these matters.[7]

Tragically, Luther adopted most of Augustine's teachings without question. He taught that salvation is entirely a matter of predestination. God arbitrarily chose some persons for eternal salvation. Others He arbitrarily chose to be eternally damned.[8] Luther even asserted that a person could not be saved if he did not believe in this doctrine of absolute, double predestination:

> "For if this is not known, there can be neither faith nor worship of God. Actually, to not know this is to be ignorant of God. And with such ignorance, salvation—it is well known—cannot consist. For if you doubt, or disdain to know, that God foreknows and wills all things, not contingently, but necessarily and unchangeably, how can you confidently believe, trust in, and depend upon His promises?...You will regard Him as neither true nor faithful—which is unbelief, the greatest of wickedness, and a denial of the Most High God!"[9]

Luther also promoted the doctrine of holy war. When German peasants rose up in revolt against the inhumane treatment they endured at the hands of the nobility, Luther recognized that their rebellion would be blamed on his teachings. So he incited the nobility to forcibly suppress the rebellion, goading them on with these words:

> Here then there is no time for sleeping; no place for patience or mercy. It is the time of the sword, not the day of grace....Any peasant who is killed is lost in body and soul and is eternally the devil's. But the rulers have a good conscience and a just cause. [They] can therefore say to God with all assurance of heart: "Behold, my God, you have

appointed me prince or lord; of this I can have no doubt. And you have committed to me the sword over the evildoers....Therefore, I will punish and smite as long as my heart beats. You will judge and make things right." Thus it may be that one who is killed while fighting on the ruler's side may be a true martyr in the eyes of God.... Strange times, these, when a prince can win heaven with bloodshed, better than other men with prayer! ...Stab, smite, slay whomever you can! If you die in doing it, well for you! A more blessed death can never be yours.[10]

The nobility followed Luther's preaching without hesitation, savagely crushing the bands of peasants in a brief conflict marked by horrible atrocities. Those peasants who weren't slain in combat were gruesomely tortured and then executed.

In short, Luther's Reformation was no return to the spirit and teachings of early Christianity. To be sure, Luther did eliminate many post-Constantinian practices in the German church, such as masses for the dead in purgatory, forced celibacy for the clergy, sale of indulgences, and religious pilgrimages as a form of "good works." By eliminating these practices, Luther did move German Christianity several steps closer to early Christianity. On the other hand, by his wholesale adoption of Augustinian theology, Luther also moved German Christianity a few steps back from early Christianity.

The Myth Of "Sola Scriptura"

Luther's most positive contribution to Western Christianity was his bold stance that there was no new special doctrinal revelation after the time of the apostles. As we saw earlier, this was also the position of the early Christians. They recognized that the church has no authority to create new theological dogmas. However, the Roman Church had begun to teach that there was continual doctrinal light given to the church through the ages. As a result, the Roman Church maintained that it had a better grasp of doctrinal truths than did the early Christians. On that basis, it added a number of doctrines to the primitive faith.

Luther rejected this claim of doctrinal revelation advanced by the Roman Church. Instead, he maintained that the Bible is our only source of authority. "Sola Scriptura"—only Scripture—became one of the banner slogans of the Reformation. However, "sola Scriptura" was a myth from the start. Nobody uses *only* Scripture as their source of authority. Rather, each person's *interpretation* of Scripture is his source of authority. Luther translated the Bible into German so the people could read it for themselves, which was a tremendous accomplishment. But at the same time, he made certain that the German people would read the Bible only through his interpretations.

Chapter 12 presented some samples from Luther's preface to the New Testament, in which he tried to direct his reader's attention away from the parts of the Bible that contradicted his theology. Luther's introduction to Romans is more than half as long as the Letter to the Romans itself. In his introduction, Luther asserted: "This Epistle is really the chief part of the New Testament and the very purest Gospel,"[11] setting Romans above the other New Testament books. He also stated, "To begin with, we must have knowledge of its language and know what St. Paul means by the words: law, sin, grace, faith, righteousness, flesh, spirit, etc. Otherwise, no reading of it has any value."[12] Luther then proceeded to define each of those terms, often in ways that were completely different from the early Christian use of those terms.

In his preface to the Epistle to the Hebrews, Luther attacked the Epistle, writing: "Again, there is a hard knot in the fact that in chapters six and ten it flatly denies and forbids to sinners repentance after baptism. And in chapter twelve it says that Esau sought repentance and did not find it. This seems, as it stands, to be against all the Gospels and St. Paul's epistles. And although one might make a gloss on it, the words are so clear that I do not know whether that would be sufficient. My opinion is that it is an epistle of many pieces put together, and it does not deal with any one subject in an orderly way."[13]

So Luther's motto of "sola Scriptura" was only a myth, since he himself took great pains to make certain that Christians didn't hear the Scriptures alone. In the final analysis, it wasn't Scripture that was the sole source of Reformation authority; it was Luther's or some other man's *interpretation* of Scripture. As someone once observed, "Before the Reformation, there was only one Pope. After the Reformation, every person with a Bible in his hand became a Pope."[14] Instead of relying upon his own personal interpretations of Scripture, or on Augustine's interpretations, Luther should have looked to the interpretations held by the primitive, undivided church. Because he didn't, the tragic result is that today there are over 22,000 denominations, sects, and independent churches—all teaching different things, yet all claiming to be teaching "only Scripture."[15]

Despite his shortcomings, Luther did make some positive contributions to the church. He was a courageous man of faith who risked his own life to bring spiritual renewal back into a lethargic church. We can admire his good qualities without having to follow his mistakes. He brought the Scriptures back into prominence and made them available to the laity. He effectively challenged the claims of the Pope as the sole head of all Christians. He steadfastly opposed the claims of the Roman Church of having new doctrinal revelation.

Most importantly, Luther paved the way for other reformers. And some of those other reformers *did* succeed in bringing parts of the church much closer to early Christianity.

16

The Radical Reformation

At about the same time that Luther began his reforms, Ulrich Zwingli was bringing reforms to the church in Switzerland. This Swiss Reformation, which was begun by Zwingli and completed by Calvin, is often referred to as the second wing of the Reformation. But there was also a third wing, that of the Anabaptists, which is often referred to as the "Radical Reformation."

The word *radical* means "of or from the roots." The Anabaptists wanted to return to the primitive roots of Christianity, even if it meant going against the tide of sixteenth century European society. Like the early church, the Anabaptists took Jesus' teachings quite literally and quite seriously. They maintained that Christians must live by the Sermon on the Mount.

For example, they generously shared their material goods with one another, providing for any needy persons among them. Although today most churches care for the needy, that wasn't the case at the time of the Reformation. Rather, at the time of the Reformation, the brotherly care extended by Anabaptists stood in stark contrast to the Lutheran, Reformed, and Roman churches around them. One Anabaptist declared to these other churches:

We teach and practice this mercy, love, and community, and we have taught and practiced it for seventeen years. God be thanked forever that although our property has to a great extent been taken away from us and is still daily taken, and many a righteous father and mother are put to the sword or fire, and although we are not allowed the free enjoyment of our homes as is manifest...Yet none of those who have joined us nor any of their orphaned children have been forced to beg. If this is not Christian practice, then we might as well abandon the whole Gospel of our Lord.

Is it not sad and intolerable hypocrisy that these poor people [the Lutherans] boast of having the Word of God, of being the true Christian church, never remembering that they have entirely lost their sign of true Christianity? Although many of them have plenty of everything, go about in silk and velvet, gold and silver, and in all manner of pomp and splendor,... they allow many of their own poor and afflicted members to ask for alms. [They force] the poor, the hungry, the suffering, the elderly, the lame, the blind, and the sick to beg for bread at their doors.

Oh preachers, dear preachers, where is the power of the Gospel you preach?...Where are the fruits of the Spirit you have received?"[1]

Like the early Christians, the Anabaptists also preached the message of the cross. "If the Head had to suffer such torture, anguish, misery, and pain, how shall His servants, children, and members expect peace and freedom as to their flesh?"[2] they asked. At the same time, although they were cruelly hunted down, tortured and executed, they refused to fight back or retaliate against their persecutors.

One of the most touching examples of their unselfish love for others is that of Dirck Willems. Fleeing from the Catholic authorities who had come to arrest him, Willems dashed across a frozen lake and made it safely to the other side. Glancing back as he ran up the banks of the shore, Willems noticed that the deputy pursuing him had fallen through the ice and was about to drown. Although he could have now escaped with ease, Willems turned back and pulled the drowning deputy to safety. Unmoved by this unselfish act of love, the officer in charge ordered the deputy to arrest Willems. As a result, Willems was apprehended, imprisoned, and eventually burned alive.

Again, like the early Christians, the Anabaptists refused to use the sword against their enemies.[3] Rather than preaching a gospel of health and wealth, they stressed simplicity of living. In fact, because of persecution, most of them lived in dire poverty.

In some respects, their theology was closer to that of the early Christians than was Luther's. For example, although "salvation by grace alone" was the slogan of the Reformation, the Anabaptists taught that *obedience* was also essential for salvation. However, they didn't teach that salvation is earned by accumulating good works, and they rejected all of the ritual works of self-justification taught by Catholics. They stressed the fact that salvation is a gift from God.

Essentially, their doctrine of salvation was identical to that of the early church. Yet because they taught that obedience is necessary for salvation, the Lutherans and Reformed Christians called them "heaven-stormers."[4] At a time when both Luther and Calvin were stressing Augustine's teachings, the Anabaptists completely rejected the doctrine of predestination. They taught instead that salvation was open to everyone, and that everyone can choose for himself either to accept or to reject God's gracious provisions for salvation.

Nevertheless, not all of the Anabaptist doctrines were identical to the early Christian beliefs. In matters such as baptism and communion, they too fell prey to "Newton's Law of Theology." Also, in their quest for holiness and separation from the world, they left no room for any unclean fish in the kingdom dragnet. They desired a dragnet with only clean fish in it. The tragic result is that they not only separated themselves from the rest of the church, but have since separated from each other. Today, the Anabaptists are fragmented into a hundred or more separate groups, most of which do not hold communion with one another.

Yet, despite their shortcomings in some areas, the Anabaptist reformation was one of the most significant movements in the history of western Christianity. Through their lives, the Anabaptists demonstrated that holiness is not something just for celibate monks and nuns. Rather, it should be the normal way of life of *all* Christians. They showed that, with God's help, whole families can live by the Sermon on the Mount.

Although the Lutheran, Reformed, and Roman Catholic churches alike cruelly persecuted the Anabaptists, God has preserved them down to this day. They stand as a powerful witness that the Sermon on the Mount is not simply some idealistic teaching that we can't take seriously. It's not something for a future dispensation, nor is it something that was only for the early church. No, it still is the way of life prescribed by Jesus for those who want to build their house on the rock.

17

The Reformation In England

Every schoolboy or girl in America learns that the Church of England was established in the sixteenth century by King Henry VIII because he wanted a divorce from his wife. Yet, despite this popular belief, that's not really how the Church of England was established.

Rather, Christianity was established in ancient Celtic Britain no later than the second century. In fact, it was probably planted in Britain by the end of the first century. For centuries thereafter the Celtic church of Britain existed as an autonomous part of the one apostolic, catholic (universal) church. It was not under the authority of the bishop of Rome or any other foreign bishop.

At the same time, the early Celtic Church was one of the most spiritually vigorous and evangelistic branches of the universal church. As has been mentioned, it not only evangelized the pagan inhabitants of the British Isles, but also sent missionaries to Europe and Africa.

Probably the most famous figure of the Celtic Church is Patrick, who lived during the early 400s. A native of Britain, he had been captured by pagan Irish raiders as a teenager and sold into slavery in Ireland. Eventually, he escaped from his captors and made his way back to Britain. However, feeling the call of God, he returned to Ireland as a missionary. With utmost faith in God, he courageously faced the opposing Druid priests, the Irish chieftains, and even his former slave master. Filled with the Holy Spirit, he journeyed throughout Ireland, preaching the Gospel and establishing churches and religious communities everywhere.

After Patrick died, an Irish nobleman named Columba became the great missionary to the Scots and Picts. Feeling remorse for a skirmish he had caused in which a few thousand men were killed, he resolved that he would win the souls of as many pagans as men who had died in that skirmish. Banishing himself from his beloved homeland of Ireland, he established a monastery on a small, barren island off of Scotland, called Iona. From here, he and his small band of monks converted most of the pagan tribes of Scotland. Through the indwelling of the Holy Spirit, Columba's fiery temper gradually melted into a spirit of gentleness, eventually earning him the nickname "the Dove."

It wasn't until almost the beginning of the seventh century that Rome sent a delegation to England to help evangelize the pagan Angles and Saxons and to bring the Celtic Church under Rome's authority. However, the Celtic Church initially rebuffed Rome's attempts to bring it under Rome's authority. Eventually, however, little by little, the Celtic Church yielded to the power of Rome. Yet, portions of the Celtic Church in Wales and Ireland remained independent of Rome until the twelfth century. Even then, their submission to Rome lasted only about four hundred years.

Henry VIII And The Reformation

So rather than *creating* the independent Church of England, what Henry VIII did was to give the native English church the opportunity to return to the autonomy it had originally enjoyed for centuries. In other words, the British church had voluntarily subjugated itself to Rome and it was now voluntarily returning to its former state of independence.

Of course, Henry's interests were personal and political, not spiritual. He remained a Roman Catholic in belief until he died. However, his break with Rome afforded the Christians in England the unique opportunity of approaching reform of the church in the calm, cautious atmosphere that was needed. Rather than hurriedly developing theological beliefs on the run as had Luther, Zwingli, and the Anabaptists, the reformers in England were able to carefully examine what the ancient, undivided church believed and then return to those beliefs. In this way, they were able to avoid "Newton's Law of Theology." Instead of throwing out the proverbial baby with the bath water, the English reformers made a conscious effort to retain what was truly catholic or apostolic and to discard what was merely Roman.

As a result, the reformation in Britain was unique in many ways. First of all, there was no single founder of the reform movement in England. There was no English Luther, Zwingli, Calvin, or Menno Simons. The tenets of the sixteenth and seventeenth century Anglican Church were not the work of some original theologian. Rather, they were the beliefs of the ancient undivided church, of which the Celtic Church had been a part.

Of course, there were *leaders* of the English Reformation, such as Archbishop Thomas Cranmer. Yet, Cranmer was no original theologian; he was a quiet scholar, well-read in the early Christian writers. He carefully sought to restore to England the primitive catholic faith it had once held to. For his efforts, he was later burned at the stake during the reign of Queen Mary.

A second unique feature about the English Reformation was that it did not produce any official confessional document comparable to the Lutheran Augsburg Confession, the Reformed Heidelberg Catechism, or the Anabaptist Dordrecht Confession. It's true that the Anglican Book of Common Prayer contains the Thirty-Nine Articles of Faith, but those have never carried the authority of the English Church. Rather, the teachings of the early, undivided church are still the rule of faith of traditional Anglicans.

This lack of a man-made creed has been one of the strong points of the Church in England. Yet, it has also given rise to numerous problems. One of these difficulties is that, from the time of Henry VIII on, there have always been two or more underlying, opposing currents within the Church of England. In the sixteenth and seventeenth centuries, the tug-of-war was between the Calvinistic Puritans and the High Churchmen, who advocated primitive catholicism. From the latter eighteenth century through the present day, the tension has been between the theological liberals and the traditionalists who want to maintain the primitive catholic faith.

The Thread Of Ancient Christianity

Despite the theological battles and the continual tug-of-war between opposing forces, the thread of ancient Christianity has remained unbroken in the English church. The faithful ones holding to this thread have often been persecuted, and have nearly always been ridiculed. Yet, with dogged determination, they have preserved the doctrines and faith of the early centuries.

One such man of determination was Jeremy Taylor (1613-1667). Educated at Cambridge, he first served as the young pastor of a village church near London. However, within a few years, the Puritan revolution of the mid-seventeenth century burst upon the scene, and England was plunged into bloody turmoil. The Puritans imprisoned Jeremy Taylor and executed his mentor, Archbishop Laud.

After his release from prison, Taylor courageously pastored parts of the underground church in England. Sometimes he served as a minister to the Anglican nobility; at other times he lived in poverty and affliction, cheerfully ministering as best he could. Despite losing his wife and several of his children during those difficult years, Taylor never lost his faith in God or his gentle spirit. He has left the church a lasting legacy in his works, *Holy Living* and *Holy Dying*.

Other such men of determination were John Jewel, Richard Hooker, William Laud, George Herbert, and Lancelot Andrewes. Unfortunately, although the Anglican torchbearers admirably preserved the doctrinal faith of the early church, they generally did not return as fully to the early Christian *lifestyle* as did the Anabaptists. Yet, some of these Anglican "divines" did rival the Anabaptists in their separation from the world and complete devotion to God.

One notable example was William Law. He abandoned a promising career at Cambridge because his conscience forbade him to swear allegiance to George I. He championed early Christian doctrine against the unorthodox, and he championed primitive holiness against the customs and entertainment of his day. His work on *Christian Perfection* deeply stirred John Wesley, and Law's *Serious Call to a Devout and Holy Life* became a classic of English spirituality.

But William Law was much more than a writer. He *lived* the things he wrote about. Through the gift of a Christian friend, he eventually established a semi-monastic community in his hometown. There he spent his days with others in prayer, Bible reading, and teaching. He vexed his neighbors by giving money without discrimination to all beggars who came to his door, whether deserving or undeserving.

During William Law's lifetime, various religious societies arose within the Church of England, composed of men, women, and families who were committed to living by Jesus' teachings. The early Methodists were one such Society within the Church of England. Their zeal for the Gospel, holiness, and care for the poor are still talked about today. Their founder, John Wesley, remained a devoted Anglican priest (presbyter) his entire life. It was not until after Wesley's death that the Methodists broke away from the Church of England and became a separate denomination.

Another well-known evangelical Anglican priest or presbyter was George Whitefield. Whitefield (1714-1770) was a tireless open-air evangelist who has been called "the greatest evangelist of the British race."[1] He preached about a thousand times a year, on both sides of the Atlantic, for thirty or more years. When a friend advised him to slow down his pace, Whitefield replied, "I had rather wear out than rust out." As one historian observed, at his death, Whitefield "had probably spoken to more people than anyone else in the world's history."[2]

The Oxford Movement

As the Church of England began to founder in spiritual lethargy and liberalism in the nineteenth century, a revival movement arose that profoundly challenged this complacency and apostasy. Begun as a crusade by clergymen and professors at Oxford University, this renewal eventually became known as the "Oxford Movement." It called for the English church to return to its ancient roots of holiness and apostolicity.

Three of the leaders of this movement were Edward Pusey, John Keble, and John Henry Newman. They launched their attack against the growing apostasy and secularism in the English church through a series of tracts. Predictably, their message earned them the scorn of their fellow professors at Oxford. But this did not deter them in the least.

As Edward Pusey wrote, "I believe that we are in the course of an inevitable revolution; that the days of the Establishment [of the English church] are numbered, and that the church has to look to [primitive] catholicism for her purity, liberty, and faithfulness."[3] One of the primary aims of the Movement was, in Pusey's words, to foster "reverence for and defense of the ancient Church" and to use the ancient Church, rather than the Reformers, as the ultimate expounder of the Scriptures.[4]

The inspiration of the Movement soon spread from Oxford into the rural districts and industrial cities of northern Britain. Having begun as an academic protest, it soon became a pastoral and evangelistic movement, accompanied by practical ministries of mercy. Leaders in the movement carried on an effective and exemplary evangelistic work in the slums of east London, Leeds, and other industrial cities.

Although ridiculed and condemned by their peers, the leaders of the Oxford Movement earned the respect of many common Englishmen. They were godly men who challenged other believers to holiness. They even spawned the birth of religious monastic societies and spiritual communities within the Anglican Church. In 1845, the Movement established the Sisterhood of the Holy Cross for women, and in 1866, it established the Society of St. John the Evangelist for men. A second sisterhood founded by the Movement was noted for its work among the poor and infirm in Plymouth and Devonport.

The men and women of the Oxford Movement shared with the earlier Anglicans a sacramental attitude towards nature and the world. They restored a sense of reverence in worship in their churches and established a pattern of regular communion for ordinary Christians. More importantly, the Movement called the church of its day to look back to the ancient church of the first four centuries. Edward Pusey personally launched a fifty volume set of translations of the early Christian writers, called the *Library of the Fathers*.

It is largely through the influence of the Oxford Movement that affordable translations of the early Christian writers are now available in English. Through their legacy, ordinary Christians like you and I can discover for ourselves what early Christianity was really like.

18

What Does All This Mean For Us?

So what does all of this mean for us? Am I suggesting that you throw out everything you've always believed and start over again? No. Rather, what I *am* suggesting is that today's evangelical church needs to face up to the early Christians.

Don't Feed Them— Maybe They'll Go Away

For the most part, evangelicals simply ignore the early Christians. We rarely talk about them in our churches, and we disregard their writings.

Our stance reminds me of the position the Pharisees took toward John the Baptist. When the Pharisees tried to trap Jesus by asking him where His authority came from, He responded by asking them where John had received his authority. The Pharisees huddled together, saying among themselves, "If we say, 'From heaven,' he will ask us why we didn't believe him. But if we say, 'From men,' the crowd will turn on us, for they all hold that John was a prophet." So they ended up answering Jesus, "We don't know" (Matt. 21:24-27).

Our approach to the early Christians is very similar. We can't say their beliefs and lifestyle were orthodox, because then we would have to acknowledge that our own beliefs and lifestyle aren't. On the other hand, we really don't want to accuse them of being heretics, because we can't deny their unconquerable faith and genuine Christian love. Furthermore, if we say they were heretics, we would have to admit that our New Testament was put together by heretics. So like the Pharisees, we refuse to take a position. We simply ignore the early Christians, as if we can somehow make them disappear by paying no attention to them. But ignoring them doesn't change the historical truths to which they bear witness.

Our Need For
Doctrinal Humility

Please understand: I'm *not* saying we should all immediately discard our beliefs and unquestioningly adopt those of the early Christians. But I am saying that we have some skeletons in our theological closet that we need to face up to. For example, many of our evangelical doctrines on salvation are nearly identical to the teachings of the gnostics. Of course, the gnostics may have been right while the church was in error. But how likely is that?

If nothing more, we all should at least be open to the *possibility* that some doctrines we consider sacred may not be correct. When I first read the early Christian writings, I painfully realized that many beliefs that I had dogmatically expounded for years were never taught by the early Christians. In fact, as I've mentioned, they specifically labeled some of my beliefs as *heretical.* To say the least, this was a rather humbling experience. But maybe we're all overdue for a strong dose of theological humility.

A short time ago, I was explaining to a Christian friend what the early Christians believed and practiced. Most of the things

I shared with him matched his own beliefs. He was quite excited about what he was hearing, feeling that the testimony of the early Christians was strong evidence that his own beliefs were correct. However, when I brought up some of their other beliefs that didn't match his own, he looked puzzled and was strangely silent for a moment. Then shaking his head in bewilderment, he somberly remarked, "*They* certainly were off base there, weren't they?" The possibility that maybe *he* was off base never even seemed to have occurred to him.

Even if we are unwilling to change our beliefs based on the testimony of the early Christians, we should (at the very least) quit being so judgmental toward others who honestly interpret the Scriptures differently than we do. Particularly if their interpretations match those of the early Christians. Jesus told us, "Do not judge or you too will be judged. For in the same way you judge others, you will be judged, and with the measure you use, it will be measured to you" (Matt. 7:1).

Many of us seem to think that Jesus didn't really mean what he said. We condemn without mercy the honest interpretations of others. And in return we think Jesus is going to give us a big smile and a pat on the back on Judgment Day. But maybe we're wrong. Maybe it's *our* interpretations that are incorrect. Maybe Jesus will do just what He said and judge us the way we have judged others.

The Early Christian Writings Give Us A Reference Point

Like many Christians, I personally believe that the Bible is the only inspired and inerrant source of authority for Christians. However, we Bible-believing Christians are now splintered into over 22,000 different denominations, sects, and independent churches.[1] Generally, the reason for these divisions is *not* that Christians have wickedly been twisting the Scriptures to suit their own purposes. Rather, it's because many teachings in the Bible aren't clear. Many Bible passages can honestly be interpreted in more than one way.

As a result, even Bible-believing Christians are forced to come up with some additional basis of authority: denominational publications, pastors, seminaries, Bible commentaries, denominational governing bodies, church conventions, creeds, and evangelical traditions. But how valuable are these secondary sources of authority? How can one seminary know more than another? How are we to say that our pastor is right and someone else's is wrong? How does a seventeenth century Bible commentator like Matthew Henry actually know what the apostles meant?

Here is where the early Christian writings could be of such invaluable help to the Bible-believing church. Those writings are not inspired, and they didn't claim to be inspired. The early Christian writers never put their works on a level anywhere near that of the Scriptures, and neither should we. However, from their writings, we *can* know what Christians believed at the close of the apostolic age. This gives us a reference point that far surpasses what any seminary, commentary, or twentieth century teacher can offer. Since we can't seem to agree on what Scriptures mean, we should perhaps be humble enough to at least listen to the interpretations of the early church—since it *was* able to agree on the essentials.

But when we use the early Christians as a point of reference, we need to be honest in our use of them. Some denominations selectively quote from the early church to bolster their own denominational viewpoints. In doing so, they argue that the testimony of the early Christians is strong evidence of what New Testament Christians believed. However, when those same denominations are confronted with other early Christian beliefs that don't match theirs, then it's different. Suddenly, what the early Christians believed is unimportant. In other words, the early Christian writings are authoritative when they match their beliefs, but they're irrelevant when they don't. Now, how honest is that? Are we really seeking God's truth when we take such an inconsistent position?

Unity On The Essentials

It is obvious from the early Christian writings that there was a core set of beliefs and practices that were handed down from the apostles. The early orthodox Christians universally accepted such essential beliefs and practices. At the same time, there were obviously many things that the apostles never explained to the church in general—nor perhaps to anyone. In those areas, there was considerable diversity of thought among the early Christians. Yet, they did not separate into a plethora of sects over such issues. In fact, there wasn't even much bickering about these matters.

For example, Justin Martyr believed that many Bible prophecies would be literally fulfilled during the Millennium. But many other early Christians believed differently. Notice the amicable spirit Justin expressed when discussing his millennial views with a group of Jews: "As I mentioned before, I and many others are of this opinion, and believe that such prophecies will take place in this manner. But, on the other hand, I told you that many who belong to the pure and righteous faith and are true Christians—think otherwise."[2] This non-belligerent, open-minded spirit was very typical of most early Christians. They did not let their diversity of views on non-essentials affect their Christian unity.

Although uncompromising in their obedience to Christ, the early Christians were very non-dogmatic on matters about which the apostles had not clearly spoken. We would do well to imitate their peaceful spirit.

Reassessing Today's Church

After studying the early Christian writings, I stepped back and re-examined my own spirituality. As I've mentioned previously, by today's standards I'm a fairly committed Christian. But by the early church standards, I'm spiritually weak. So I had to ask myself, "How does *God* view me?"

Perhaps the entire church needs to ask itself this same question. How does God view the church today? Is He smiling with favor on us and showering us with blessings—or does He view us as a worldly, apostate church? If Jesus were writing a letter to the church today, would He say to us what He told the church in Smyrna, "I know your afflictions and your poverty—yet you are rich!"? Or, would He repeat his words to the church in Laodicea, "You say, 'I am rich; I have acquired wealth and do not need a thing.' But you do not realize that you are wretched, pitiful, poor, blind and naked" (Rev. 2:9;3:17).

Today many Christians are claiming that we are living in a new era of the church, that God has begun to shower the church with material prosperity, miracles, and other blessings that were somehow withheld from the church during the past two thousand years.

Of course, it's possible that, for some reason, God is showering special blessings on the church of today. But based on the record of past history, I think it's highly unlikely that He is doing so. It's far more likely that we are simply deceiving ourselves. After all, why would God make the faithful Christians of the early church carry their cross of suffering, while He showers the Christians of today with material prosperity, miraculous health, and other fleshly gratifications? Please don't misunderstand me. I'm not denying that God performs miracles. There are records of miracles and miraculous healing in the early church. But those were unusual occurrences, and they weren't the primary emphasis of the church.

Churches today that emphasize material blessings, healings, and miracles are growing at an explosive rate. But is such growth really evidence of God's approval? Remember, the church grew nearly ten times as fast *after* Constantine's conversion, than before. Yet, it did not grow in holiness, only in numbers. Jesus forewarned us, "Many will say to me on that day, 'Lord, Lord, did we not prophesy in your name, and in your name drive out demons and perform many miracles?' Then I will tell them plainly, 'I never knew you. Away from me, you evil-doers'" (Matt. 7:22,23).

Even among more traditional evangelicals, church growth has become an obsession. Methods that produce rapid church growth are soon adopted by church after church. For example, the big rage right now where I live is multi-million-dollar church recreation complexes, called "family life" centers. From what I've observed, churches with expensive recreation centers grow much faster than those without. But so what? The fourth century church proved that we can successfully use human methods to create a bigger church. But the fourth century church did not prove that we can use human means to create a *better* church.

It's Not Too Late To Return

Christianity was originally a revolution that challenged the attitudes, lifestyle, and values of the ancient world. It was more than a mere set of doctrines—it was an entire way of life. And all the military, economic, and social forces of the Roman world couldn't stop it. But after 300 years, the revolution partially foundered.

It ran aground because most professing Christians lost their obedient trust in God. They imagined they could improve Christianity through human means, by adopting the methods of the world. But they didn't improve Christianity; they gutted it.

There's a down-to-earth saying in rural Texas: "If it's not broken, don't fix it." In other words, don't try to improve something if there's nothing wrong with it. The "improvement" usually ends up being something worse.

There was nothing wrong with early Christianity. It didn't need "fixing." But the fourth century Christians became convinced that they could improve Christianity. "If Christianity meant material blessings and prosperity instead of suffering and deprivation, we could convert the whole world," they reasoned. But in the end, the church didn't really convert the world. The world converted much of the church.

Yet, somehow the lessons of history have failed to convince Christians today. The church is still married to the world, and Christians still think they can improve Christianity through human means. But Christianity will not *improve* until the church returns to the simple holiness, genuine love, and cross-bearing of the early Christians. Our divorce from the world is long overdue, and this is one divorce that would have God's unequivocal blessings.

The cross and revolutionary banner of early Christianity are still lying where the early martyrs left them. It's not too late for the church to return and carry them again.

Biographical Dictionary

Alexander (AL ig ZAN der) *273-326.* Bishop of the church at Alexandria, Egypt, at the outbreak of the Arian controversy that sharply divided the church and led to the Council of Nicea. He strongly opposed the views of Arius.

Apollonius (AP o LO nee us) *175-225.* Writer of a short work against the Montanists. Little else is known about him.

Archelaus (AR keh LAY us) *250-300.* Church bishop who publicly debated a gnostic teacher named Manes, a record of which debate has been preserved.

Arius (AIR ee us) *270-336.* Presbyter in the church at Alexandria who disputed with Alexander over the nature of Christ. Arius taught that Jesus was of a different nature than the Father, which view was condemned at the Council of Nicea.

Arnobius (ar NO bee us) *260-303.* Christian apologist who wrote shortly before the reign of Constantine. Lactantius was one of his pupils.

Athanasius (ATH ah NAY shee us) *300-373.* Bishop of Alexandria after the death of Alexander. He wrote several theological treatises and was the champion defender of the Nicene Creed.

Athenagoras (a THEN a GOR us) *150-190.* Christian apologist who had been a Greek philosopher before his conversion. His apology was presented to Emperors Marcus Aurelius and Commodus about 177 A.D.

Augustine (AW gus teen *or* aw GUS tin) *354-430.* Bishop of the church at Hippo, North Africa, and father of Western theology.

Barnabas (BAR nah bus) *prior to 150.* Writer of a general letter widely circulated among the early Christians. He may have been the same person as the well-known companion of the apostle Paul, but this is disputed by most scholars.

Caius (KAY us *or* Ki us) *180-217.* Presbyter in the church at Rome who wrote several works against major heresies of his day.

Calvin, John (KAL vin) *1509-1564.* French theologian and preacher who settled in Geneva, Switzerland, and became the leader of the

Reformation already in progress there. He is the Father of the Reformed churches and of Presbyterian doctrine.

Celsus (SELL sus) *125-175.* Pagan Roman philosopher who wrote a blistering attack on Christianity, which was later brilliantly answered by Origen.

Clement of Rome (KLEM ent) *30-100.* First century bishop of the church at Rome and evidently a companion of both Peter and Paul (Phil. 4:3). He wrote a letter to the Corinthians sometime near the end of the first century.

Clement of Alexandria (KLEM ent) *150-200.* Presbyter in the church at Alexandria, Egypt, who was in charge of the school of instruction there for new Christians. Origen was one of his pupils.

Constantine (KON stan teen) *274-337.* Roman general who became ruler of the western half of the Roman Empire in 312 and attributed his victory over his rival to the God of the Christians. He issued the Edict of Milan in 313, giving Christianity legal recognition for the first time. He convened the Council of Nicea in 325.

Cyprian (SIP ree an) *200-258.* Bishop of the church in Carthage, North Africa, during a period of fierce persecution. He shepherded his congregation underground for a decade before being captured and executed by the Romans. Many of the letters written by, and to, him have been preserved.

Edict of Milan (ME lawn) *313.* Decree issued jointly by Constantine and Licinius, rulers of the western and eastern halves of the Roman Empire, giving legal recognition to Christianity for the first time.

Eusebius (you SEE bee us) *270-340.* Bishop of the church in Caesarea during the time of Constantine's reign. He wrote a complete history of the church, tracing Christianity from the days of Jesus through the reign of Constantine.

Felix, Mark Minucius (meh NEW shus FEE licks) *170-215.* Roman lawyer who converted to Christianity. He wrote one of the finest apologies of early Christianity, written in the form of a dialogue between a Christian and a pagan. He is cited herein simply as "Mark Felix."

gnostics (NOSS ticks) The predominant group of heretics during the period of the early church. Gnosticism began during the time of the apostle John and continued under various names well into the Middle Ages. Although there were many different schools of thought among the gnostics, there were several tenets that characterized them all such as (1) claims of special knowledge *(gnosis)* from God, (2) the belief that humans were created by an inferior god, who was not the Father of Jesus, and (3) that the Son of God did not truly become man.

Gregory of Nazianzus (NAZ ee AN zus) *325-391.* Fourth century theologian who is often designated as one of the three "Cappadocian fathers." He wrote several treatises on the person of the Holy Spirit and was instrumental in shaping Christian doctrine on the Trinity.

Hermas (HUR mus) *prior to 150.* Author of an allegorical work entitled *The Shepherd,* which was widely read and held in great esteem by many early Christian churches. Some of the early Christians believed the author to be the same person referred to by Paul in Romans 16:14, but their testimony cannot be verified.

Hippolytus (hih POL ih tus) *170-236.* Church leader, writer, martyr, and pupil of Irenaeus. His most important work is entitled *The Refutation of All Heresies.*

Ignatius (ig NAY shus *or* ig NAY she us) *50-100.* Bishop of the church at Antioch and a personal disciple of the Apostle John. He was executed near the end of the first century.

Irenaeus (EAR eh NAY us) *120-205.* Bishop of the church at Lyons, France, and a pupil of Polycarp.

Justin Martyr (JUS tin) *110-165.* Philosopher who converted to Christianity and became a tireless evangelist. His works are the earliest Christian apologies in existence. He was executed during the reign of Marcus Aurelius, about 165.

Lactantius (lack TAN she us) *260-330.* Prominent Roman teacher of rhetoric, who later converted to Christianity. He settled in France, where he became the teacher of Constantine's son. His principal Christian work is entitled *Introduction to True Religion,* or *The Divine Institutes.*

Luther, Martin (LU ther) *1483-1546.* German monk who began the Reformation. Although his original dispute with the Roman Catholic Church was only over the sale of indulgences, he eventually challenged Rome on many issues, such as the doctrine of salvation, the authority of Scripture, the use of images and religious relics, and private Masses for the dead. He is the father of Lutheran and evangelical theology.

Marcion (MAR she on *or* MAR see on) *110-165.* Prominent gnostic teacher of the second century, who formed his own church and formulated his own New Testament.

Methodius (meh THO dee us) *260-315.* Overseer of Tyre and martyr, who wrote against some of the excessive speculations of Origen.

Montanists (MON tah nists) Sect who called themselves the "New Prophecy" movement, but were labeled as "Montanists" by the church, after their founder Montanus. They claimed that the Paraclete or Holy Spirit was still giving new ordinances to the church. Members of this group often prophesied while in uncontrolled emotional frenzies.

Origen (OR ih jen) *185-255.* Teacher in the church at Alexandria, Egypt, and the first writer of Bible commentaries. He was a pupil of Clement of Alexandria, and he took over the school there for new believers after the departure of Clement.

Pelagius (peh LAY jee us) *360-420.* British monk and traveling evangelist who stressed man's works and free will almost to the exclusion of the role of grace in salvation. His teachings were strongly attacked by Augustine.

Polycarp (POL ih karp) *69-156.* Bishop of the church at Smyrna and a companion of the apostle John. He was arrested in his very old age and burned to death.

Simons, Menno (MEN o SI mons) *1492-1559.* Dutch Roman Catholic priest who joined the Anabaptist movement and eventually became its leading writer and spokesman.

Tertullian (tur TULL yen) *140-230.* Leader in the church at Carthage, North Africa, and one of the few early Christians who wrote in Latin. He wrote numerous apologies, works against heretics, and exhortations to other Christians. He later joined a branch of the Montanist sect.

Tetzel, Johann (TET sell) *1465-1519.* Dominican friar and enthusiastic seller of indulgences. Martin Luther took issue with his claims concerning indulgences, which confrontation ignited the Reformation in Germany.

Note: Dates for the pre-Nicene writers are approximate.

Notes

Chapter 1
* The scene portrayed in this chapter is taken from the *Letter from the Church* of *Smyrna* concerning the martyrdom of Polycarp.

Chapter 2
1. Another term I should briefly define is "Romans." When I speak of the Romans in this book, I'm using the term broadly to refer to all pagan citizens of the Roman Empire, not merely to the people whose national origin was in Rome or Italy.
2. Irenaeus *Against Heresies* bk. 3, chap. 3.
3. Justin, *Conversation with Trypho* chap. 8, *paraphrased*.
4. In the alternative, Tertullian may have served as a presbyter in the congregation at Rome, before he moved to Carthage.

Chapter 3
1. Unknown author *Letter to Diognetus* chap. 5.
2. Justin *First Apology* chap. 11.
3. Untitled homily ascribed to Clement chaps. 5, 6.
4. Cyprian *Letter to Donatus* sec. 14.
5. M. Felix *Octavius* chaps. 8,12.
6. Tertullian *Apology* chap. 39.
7. Justin *First Apology* chap. 14.
8. Clement *Miscellanies* bk. 7, chap. 12.
9. Eusebius *History of the Church* bk. 7, chap. 22.
10. Cyprian *Letter To Euchratius* (epis. 60).
11. M. Felix *Octavius* chap. 31.
12. Tertullian *Apology* chap. 39; Clement *Miscellanies* bk. 7, chap. 12.
13. Lactantius *Divine Institutes* bk. 6, chap. 10.
14. Clement *Miscellanies* bk. 4, chap. 7.
15. M. Felix *Octavius* chap. 38.
16. Clement *Miscellanies* bk. 5, chap. 1.
17. M. Felix *Octavius* chap. 18, *paraphrased*.
18. Origen *Against Celsus* bk. 8, chap. 70.
19. *Ibid.,* chap. 68.

Chapter 4
1. Tertullian *To the Nations* bk. 2, chap. 1.
2. Tertullian *Apology* chap. 6.
3. Hermas *The Shepherd* bk. 2, Comm. 4, chap. 1.

4. Origen *Commentary on Matthew* bk. 14, chap. 17, *paraphrased.*
5. Justin *First Apology* chap. 15; Athenagoras *Embassy* chap. 33.
6. Cynthia Scott, 'Divorce Dilemma," *Moody Monthly* (September, 1981): 7.
7. M. Felix *Octavius* chap. 30.
8. Athenagoras *Embassy* chap. 35.
9. Tertullian *Apology* chap. 9.
10. Charles Panati, *Extraordinary Origins of Everyday Things,* (New York: Harper & Row, 1987), p. 223.
11. Clement *The Instructor* bk. 2, chap. 11, *paraphrased.*
12. *Ibid.*
13. Clement *Instructor* bk. 3, chap. 5; Cyprian *On the Dress of Virgins* chap. 19; *Constitution of the Holy Apostles* bk. 1, sec. 3, chap. 9.
14. Clement *Instructor* bk. 3, chap. 5.
15. *Ibid.;* Cyprian *Dress of Virgins.*
16. Lactantius *Institutes* bk. 6, chap. 20, *paraphrased.*
17. Tertullian *The Shows* chaps. 21, 17.
18. Lactantius *Institutes* bk. 6, chap. 20, *paraphrased.*
19. Arnobius *Against the Pagans* bk. 1, chap. 31.
20. Lactantius *Institutes* bk. 6, chap. 10.
21. Origen wrote, "[Celsus] gives credence to the histories of barbarians and Greeks respecting the antiquity of those nations of whom he speaks. But he stamps the histories of this nation alone [Israel] as being false.... Observe at once, then, the arbitrary procedure of this individual, who believes the histories of these nations on the ground of their being learned, and condemns others as being ignorant.... It seems, then, to be not from a love of truth, but from a spirit of hatred, that Celsus makes these statements, his object being to disparage the origin of Christianity, which is connected with Judaism.... The Egyptians, then, when they boastfully give their own account of the divinity of animals, are to be considered wise. But if any Jew, who has signified his adherence to the law and the Lawgiver, refers everything to the Creator of the universe—and the only God—he is, in the opinion of Celsus and those like him, deemed inferior." Origen *Against Celsus* bk. 1, chaps. 14-20.
22. Clement *Instructor* bk. 2, chap. 13.
23. Lactantius *Institutes* bk. 5, chaps. 15, 16.
24. Bart Winer, *Life in the Ancient World* (New York: Random House, Inc., 1961), p. 176.
25. M. Felix *Octavius* chap. 24.
26. Tertullian *Prescription Against Heretics* chap. 41.
27. M. Felix *Octavius* chap. 16.
28. Clement *Instructor* bk. 1, chap. 4.

Chapter 5.
1. John Donne, *Devotions.*

2. Cyprian On *the Unity of the Church* sec. 5.
3. Clement *Maximus, Sermon 55.*
4. M. Felix *Octavius* chaps. 8,12; Tertullian *The Shows* chaps. 20, 24.
5. Tertullian *Apology* chap. 39.
6. Lactantius *Institutes* bk. 4, chap. 23.
7. Cyprian *Letter to the Congregation in Spain* (epis. 67, chaps. 4, 5).
8. Cyprian *Letter to the Congregation in Furni* (epis. 65).
9. Hermas *The Shepherd* bk. 2, comm. 11; Clement *Miscellanies* bk. 1, chap. 1; Apollonius *Against Montanus;* Tertullian *Heretics* chap. 41.
10. Lactantius *Institutes* bk. 7, chap. 5.
11. Ignatius *Letter to the Magnesians* chap. 5.
12. Ignatius *Letter to the Romans* chap. 5.
13. Tertullian *To the Martyrs* chaps. 2, 3.
14. Tertullian *Apology* chap. 50.
15. Menno Simons, a contemporary of Martin Luther, gave this brief description of Lutheran Germany at the peak of the Reformation: "Let everyone take heed how he [Martin Luther] teaches. For with this same doctrine they [the Lutherans] have led the reckless and ignorant people, great and small, city dweller and cottager alike, into such a fruitless, unregenerate life, and have given them such a free rein, that one would scarcely find such an ungodly and abominable life among Turks and Tartars as among these people. Their open deeds bear testimony, for the abundant eating and drinking; the excessive pomp and splendor; the fornicating, lying, cheating, cursing; the swearing by the wounds of the Lord, by the sacraments and the sufferings of the Lord; the shedding of blood; [and] the fightings." Menno Simons, *The Complete Writings of Menno Simons.* Trans. J. C. Wenger: *True Christian Faith* (Scottdale, Pa: Herald Press, 1956) p. 333. Lutheran pastors and secular historians have painted a similar picture. See for example, Philip Jacob Spener, *Pia Desideria.*
16. Hermas *The Shepherd* bk. 2, comm. 12, chap. 4.
17. Origen *Against Celsus* bk. 7, chap. 42.
18. Clement *Salvation of the Rich Man* chap. 21.
19. Origen *Of First Things* bk. 3, chap. 1, sec. 5.
20. Clement *Rich Man* chap. 25.
21. Lactantius *Institutes* bk. 5, chap. 13.

Chapter 6:

1. Francis A. Schaeffer, *How Should We Then Live?* (Old Tappan, NJ: Fleming H. Revell Company, 1976), pp. 31, 32.
2. "In the twelfth year of the same reign Clement succeeded Anencletus after the latter had been overseer of the church of Rome for twelve years. The apostle in his Epistle to the Philippians informs us that this Clement was his fellow-worker. His words are as follows: 'With Clement and the rest of my fellow workers, whose names are in the book of life.' There is extant an epistle of this Clement which is ac-

knowledged to be genuine." Eusebius *History of the Church* bk. 3, chaps. 15,16.

Irenaeus wrote about Clement, "This man, as he had seen the blessed apostles, and had been conversant with them, might be said to have the preaching of the apostles still echoing [in his ears], and their traditions before his eyes." Irenaeus *Heresies* bk. 3, chap. 3, sec. 3.

Clement of Alexandria treated the *Letter to the Corinthians* by Clement of Rome as Scripture and referred to the writer as "the apostle Clement." Clement of Alexandria, *Miscellanies* bk. 4, chap. 17.

Origen describes Clement as "a disciple of the apostles." Origen *First Things* bk. 2, chap. 3, sec. 6.

"(A. D. 30-100) Clement was probably a Gentile and a Roman. He seems to have been at Philippi with St. Paul (A.D. 57) when that first-born of the Western churches was passing through great trials of faith." A. Cleveland Coxe, *The Ante-Nicene Fathers,* vol. 1, *Introductory Note to the First Epistle of Clement to the Corinthians* (Grand Rapids: Wm. B. Eerdmans Publishing Company, 1985), p. 1.

"Clement, a name of great celebrity in antiquity, was a disciple of Paul and Peter, to whom he refers as the chief examples for imitation." Philip Schaff, *History of the Christian Church,* vol. 2 (Grand Rapids: Wm. B. Eerdmans Publishing Company, 1910), p. 637.

3.   Clement of Rome *Letter to the Corinthians* chaps. 34, 35.
4.   Polycarp *Letter to the Philippians* chap. 2.
5.   Barnabas *Letter* of *Barnabas* chap. 21.
6.   Hermas *Shepherd* bk. 2, comm. 7; bk. 3, sim. 10, chap. 2.
7.   Justin *First Apology* chap. 10.
8.   Clement *Exhortation to the Heathen* chap. 11.
9.   Clement *Rich Man* chaps. 1, 2.
10. Origen *Of First Things* preface, chap. 5.
11. Hippolytus *Fragments from Commentaries* "On Proverbs."
12. Hippolytus *Against Plato* sec. 3.
13. Cyprian *Unity of the Church* sec. 15.
14. Lactantius *Institutes* bk. 7, chap. 5.
15. Clement of Rome *Corinthians* chap. 32.
16. Polycarp *Philippians* chap. 1.
17. Barnabas *Letter* chap 5.
18. Justin *Trypho* chap. 111.
19. Clement *Miscellanies* bk. 6, chap. 13.
20. *Ibid.,* bk. 1, chap. 7.
21. Josh McDowell, *Evidence that Demands a Verdict* (San Bernadino, Ca: Here's Life Publishers, Inc., 1972) pp. 50-52.
22. Irenaeus *Against Heresies* bk. 4, chap. 27, sec. 2.
23. Tertullian *On Repentance* chap. 6.
24. Cyprian *Unity of the Church* sec. 21.
25. Tertullian *On the Resurrection of the Flesh* chap. 4; *Against the Valentinians* chaps. 24-30; *Against Marcion* bk. 1, chaps. 2, 13, 17-

21; Irenaeus *Against Heresies* bk. 1, chaps. 5, 6, 24-27; bk. 4, chaps. 28, 29.

26. Other Scriptures cited by the early Christians were: "If you keep my commandments, you will abide in my love." (John 15:10 RSV); "If you hold to my teachings, you are really my disciples." (John 8:31); "If any one keeps my word, he will never see death." (John 8:51 RSV); "He will put the sheep on his right and the goats on his left. Then the King will say to those on his right, 'Come, you who are blessed by my Father; take your inheritance, the kingdom prepared for you since the creation of the world. For I was hungry and you gave me something to eat, I was thirsty and you gave me something to drink.'" (Matt. 25:33-35). I am the true vine, and my Father is the gardener. He cuts off every branch in me that bears no fruit.... If anyone does not remain in me, he is like a branch that is thrown away and withers; such branches are picked up, thrown into the fire and burned." (John 15:1,6); "For he will render to every man according to his works: to those who by patience in well-doing seek for glory and honor and immortality, he will give eternal life." (Rom. 2:6,7 RSV); "By this gospel you are saved, if you hold firmly to the word I preached to you. Otherwise, you have believed in vain." (I Cor. 15:2); "See to it that you do not refuse him who speaks. If they did not escape when they refused him who warned them on earth, how much less will we, if we turn away from him who warns us from heaven?" (Heb. 12:25); "Blessed is the man who endures trial, for when he stands the test, he will be given the crown of life, which God has promised to those who love him." (Jas. 1:12 GSP).

Chapter 7

1. Martin Luther, *The Bondage of the Will,* trans. Henry Cole (Grand Rapids: Baker Book House, 1976), p. 70.
2. Justin *First Apology* chap. 43.
3. Clement *Miscellanies* bk. 1, chap. 17.
4. Archelaus *Disputation With Manes* secs. 32, 33.
5. Methodius *The Banquet of the Ten Virgins* discourse 8, chap. 16.
6. Luther, *Bondage,* pp. 43, 44.
7. Origen *First Things* bk. 3, chap. 1, *paraphrased and abridged.*

Chapter 8

1. Irenaeus *Heresies* bk. 1, chap. 21, sec. 1.
2. Justin *Trypho* chap. 44.
3. Irenaeus *Fragments from Lost Writings,* no. 34.
4. Clement *Instructor* bk. 1, chap. 6.
5. Cyprian *To Donatus* sec. 3.
6. Tertullian *On Repentance* chap. 6.
7. Justin *First Apology* chap. 61.

Chapter 9

1. Dr. Paul Yonggi Cho, *Salvation, Health and Prosperity* (Altamonte Springs, Fl: Creation House, 1987), p. 51.
2. Hermas *Shepherd* bk. 1, vis. 3, chap. 6.
3. *Ibid.,* bk. 3, sim. 4.
4. Clement *Rich Man* sec. 1.
5. Cyprian *On the Lapsed* secs. 11, 12, *paraphrased.*
6. Lactantius *Institutes* bk. 6, chap. 4, *paraphrased.*
7. M. Felix *Octavius* chap. 12.
8. *Ibid.,* chap. 36.
9. Origen *Against Celsus* bk. 7, chap. 18.
10. Kenneth Hagin, *How God Taught Me About Prosperity* (Tulsa: RHEMA Bible Church, 1985), pp. 17-19. Author's italics have been omitted.
11. Eusebius *History* bk. 7, chap. 30.
12. Cyprian On *Mortality,* sec. 8, *paraphrased.*

Chapter 10

1. John Calvin, *Treatises Against the Anabaptists and Against the Libertines,* trans. Benjamin Wirt Farley (Grand Rapids: Baker Book House, 1982), p. 77, 78.
2. Clement *Miscellanies* bk. 7, chap. 8.
3. Tertullian *On Idolatry* chap. 11.
4. "There are commandments contained in the Gospel which admit of no doubt whether they are to be observed according to the letter or not, such as . . . 'But I say unto you, swear not at all.'" Origen *Of First Things* bk. 4, chap. 1, sec. 19. See also Cyprian *On Mortality* chap. 4 and Eusebius *History* bk. 6, chap. 5.
5. Justin *First Apology* chap. 39.
6. Tertullian *The Crown* chap. 11.
7. Origen *Against Celsus* bk. 3, chap. 7.
8. Cyprian *To Donatus* sec. 6.
9. Arnobius *Against the Heathen* bk. 1, sec. 6.
10. Origen *Against Celsus* bk. 8, chap. 73.
11. *Ibid.,* bk. 2, chap. 30.
12. See Tertullian *Apology* chaps. 5, 42; Eusebius *History* bk. 6, chap. 5; bk. 7, chap. 11.
13. Lactantius *Institutes* bk. 6, chap. 20.

Chapter 11

1. Tertullian *Against Marcion* bk. 4, chap. 4, *paraphrased.*
2. Clement of Rome, *Corinthians* chaps. 5, 44. (See also Chapter 6, fn. 2, *supra).*

Chapter 12

1. Tertullian *Prescription Against Heretics* chaps. 6, 21.
2. Irenaeus *Heresies* bk. 3, preface and chap. 1.

3. "These things are recorded in regard to James, who is said to be the author of the first of the so-called catholic epistles. But it is to be observed that it is disputed; at least, not many of the ancients have mentioned it." Eusebius *History* bk. 2, chap. 23.
4. Luther, *Works of Martin Luther—The Philadelphia Edition,* trans. C. M. Jacobs, vol. 6: *Preface to the New Testament* (Grand Rapids: Baker Book House, 1982), pp. 439-444.
5. Archelaus *Manes* chap. 40.
6. The church of the third century was more tightly structured than that of the second. Also, the role of the bishop had grown in importance and that of the body of presbyters had declined somewhat.
7. Irenaeus *Heresies* bk. 3, chap. 4, sec. 1.
8. Tertullian *Heretics* chaps. 27, 28, *paraphrased.*

Chapter 13

1. Samuel Johnson, Boswell's *Life* of *Johnson,* vol. 1, p. 348.
2. Eusebius *History* bk. 8, chap 1.
3. Eusebius *The Life of Constantine* bk. 1, chap. 28.
4. See Origen *Against Celsus* bk. 8, chaps. 24, 55, etc.
5. Eusebius *History* bk. 10, chap. 5.
6. *Ibid.,* chaps. 5, 7.
7. Eusebius *Constantine* bk. 2, chap. 44; bk. 4, chap. 56.
8. Socrates *History of the Church* bk. 2, chap. 13. See also bk. 1, chap. 24.
9. Eusebius *Constantine* bk. 3, chaps. 64, 65, *paraphrased.*

Chapter 14

1. Philip Schaff, *History of the Christian Church*, vol. 5 (Grand Rapids: Wm. B. Eerdmans Publishing Company, 1910), p. 407.

Chapter 15

1. Luther, *Works of Martin Luther—The Philadelphia Edition,* trans. C. M. Jacobs, vol. 1: *Letter to the Archbishop Albrecht of Mainz* (Grand Rapids: Baker Book House, 1982), p. 26.
2. Augustine *The City of God* bk. 1, chap. 21.
3. Augustine *The Correction of the Donatists* Chap 5.
4. Augustine On *Forgiveness of Sins and Baptism of Infants* bk. 1, chap. 21.
5. Augustine *On the Predestination of the Saints.*
6. *Ibid.*
7. *Ibid.*
8. Luther, *Bondage of the Will,* pp. 38-45,171-174.
9. *Ibid., p.* 44.
10. Luther, *Works of Martin Luther—The Philadelphia Edition,* trans. C. M. Jacobs, vol. 4: *Against the Robbing and Murdering Peasants,* pp. 252, 253.

11. *Ibid.,* vol. 6: *Preface to Romans,* p. 447.
12. *Ibid.*
13. *Ibid.,* vol. 6: *Preface to Hebrews,* pp. 476, 477.
14. Jordan Bajis, *Common Ground,* (Minneapolis: Light and Life Publishing Company, 1991), p. 48.
15. Jeffery L. Sheler, "Reuniting the flock," *U. S. News & World Report,* March 4, 1991, p. 50.

Chapter 16
1. Menno Simons, *The Complete Writings of Menno Simons.* Trans. J. C. Wenger: *Reply to False Accusations* (Scottdale, Pa: Herald Press, 1956) pp. 558, 559.
2. *Ibid., Foundation of Christian Doctrine,* pp. 109, 110.
3. *Ibid., Reply to False Accusations,* p. 555; *Foundation of Christian Doctrine,* p. 175.
4. *Ibid., Reply to False Accusations,* p. 566.

Chapter 17
1. David L. Edwards, *Christian England,* vol. 3 ((Grand Rapids: Wm. B. Eerdmans Publishing Company, 1984), p. 50.
2. *Ibid.*
3. *Ibid.,* p. 182.
4. *Ibid.,* p. 181.

Chapter 18
1. Jeffery L. Sheler, "Reuniting the flock," *U. S. News & World Report,* March 4, 1991, p. 50.
2. Justin *Trypho* chap. 80, *paraphrased.*

Works Cited

All quotations from the pre-Nicene Christians are taken from: Roberts, Alexander and Donaldson, James, eds. *The AnteNicene Fathers.* 10 vols. Grand Rapids: Wm. B. Eerdmans Publishing Company, 1985.

All quotations from Eusebius, Socrates, and other early post-Nicene writers (except Augustine) are taken from: Schaff, Philip and Wace, Henry, eds., *The Nicene and Post-Nicene Fathers, Second Series.* 10 vols. Grand Rapids: Wm. B. Eerdmans Publishing Company, 1982.

All quotations from Augustine are taken from: Schaff, Philip, ed. *The Nicene and Post-Nicene Fathers, First Series.* 10 vols. Grand Rapids: Wm. B. Eerdmans Publishing Company, 1983.

All quotations from Martin Luther, except for those from *The Bondage of the Will,* are taken from: Luther, Martin. *Works of Martin Luther—The Philadelphia Edition.* 6 vols. Translated by C. M. Jacobs. Grand Rapids: Baker Book House, 1982.

All quotations from Menno Simons are from: Simons, Menno. *The Complete Writings of Menno Simons.* Translated by J. C. Wenger. Scottdale, Pa: Herald Press. 1956.

One notable characteristic of early Greek and Latin writers (and some of the German) is that they wrote in extremely long sentences. Sometimes one sentence fills an entire page. Where possible, for the sake of readability, I have divided these long sentences into two or more shorter sentences. Also, I have substituted common English equivalents for archaic or academic words used by the translators. Finally, in place of the term "bishop," I have sometimes used the more familiar evangelical term "overseer."

Unless indicated otherwise, all Bible quotations are from the New International Version, published by Zondervan Publishing House. Bible quotations followed by "NAS" are from the New American Standard Bible, published by Thomas Nelson Publishers. Bible quotations followed by "GSP" are from An American Translation by Edgar J. Goodspeed, published by The University of Chicago Press.

Bible quotations followed by "RSV" are from the Revised Standard Version, published by Thomas Nelson Publishers.

Other works cited are:

Bajis, Jordan. *Common Ground.* Minneapolis: Light and Life Publishing Company, 1990.

Cairns, Earle E. *Christianity Through the Centuries.* Grand Rapids: Zondervan Publishing House, 1954.

Calvin, John. *Treatises Against the Anabaptists and Against the Libertines.* Translated by Benjamin Wirt Farley. Grand Rapids: Baker Book House, 1982.

Calvin, John. *Institutes of the Christian Religion.* 2 vols. Translated by Henry Beveridge. Grand Rapids: Wm. B. Eerdmans Publishing Company, 1983.

Cho, Paul Yonggi. *Salvation, Health and Prosperity.* Altamonte Springs, Fl: Creation House, 1987.

Edwards, David L. *Christian England.* 3 vols. Grand Rapids: William B. Eerdmans Publishing Co., 1984.

Gonzalez, Justo. *A History of Christian Thought.* 3 vols. Nashville: Abingdon Press, 1970.

Hagin, Kenneth. *How God Taught Me About Prosperity.* Tulsa: RHEMA Bible Church, 1985.

Luther, Martin. *The Bondage of the Will.* Translated by Henry Cole. Grand Rapids: Baker Book House, 1976.

McDowell, Josh. *Evidence that Demands a Verdict.* San Bernadino, Ca.: Here's Life Publishers, Inc., 1972.

Panati, Charles. *Extraordinary Origins of Everyday Things.* New York: Harper & Row, 1987.

Schaeffer, Francis A. *How Should We Then Live?* Old Tappan, NJ: Fleming H. Revell Company, 1976.

Schaff, Philip. *History of the Christian Church.* 8 vols. Grand Rapids: Wm. B. Eerdmans Publishing Company, 1910.

Spener, Philip Jacob. *Pia Desideria.* Translated by Theodore G. Tappert. Philadelphia: Fortress Press, 1964.

Winer, Bart. *Life in the Ancient World.* New York: Random House, Inc., 1961.

If you enjoyed this book, you will want to read . . .

Common Sense

A New Approach to Understanding Scripture

David W. Bercot

In this hard-hitting and controversial sequel to *Will The Real Heretics Please Stand Up*, Bercot develops in more detail some of the themes introduced in the *Heretics* book and drops some more bombshells on his readers. This is definitely a book for truth-seekers only.

To order your copy, and to obtain a free catalog of other works published by Scroll Publishing Company, write P. O. Box 6175, Tyler, TX 75711, or call (903) 597-8023.

"A friend loaned me his copy of Common Sense. Great job! I've never read a book that could step on everyone's toes in such a sweet spirit. I want to order two copies."

Conroe, Texas

Free catalog for the do-it-yourself Christian historical sleuth

This book has discussed only a handful of the beliefs and practices of the early Christians. There is so much more to learn from them. Think for a minute about some of the questions Christians have been arguing about for centuries:

- What is the significance of 666, the number of the wild beast in Revelation? What is "Babylon, the mother of harlots" which is referred to in Revelation?
- Did miraculous gifts of the Spirit continue after the death of the apostles?
- What did Jesus mean when he referred to the wine and bread of the Last Supper, as "my blood and my body"?

Answers to these and many other questions are in the early Christian writings. The best way to find these answers is to read the early Christian writings for yourself.